DANGEROUS PRECINCTS

Dangerous Precincts

The Mystery of the Wakeford Case

John Treherne

JONATHAN CAPE
THIRTY-TWO BEDFORD SQUARE LONDON

To Paul Chipchase
who first told me about Wakeford

First published 1987
Reprinted 1988
Copyright © 1987 by John Treherne
Jonathan Cape Ltd, 32 Bedford Square, London WC1B 3EL

British Library Cataloguing in Publication Data

Treherne, John
Dangerous precincts: the mystery of the
Wakeford case.
1. Church of England — England — Kirkstead
(Lincolnshire) — History — 20th century
2. Kirkstead (Lincolnshire) — Church history
I. Title
283′.42532   BX5110.K/
ISBN 0-224-02378-0

Printed in Great Britain by
Butler & Tanner Ltd, Frome and London

CONTENTS

ILLUSTRATIONS

LINE ILLUSTRATIONS

'No law-suit of modern times has aroused wider public interest or stirred deeper human feelings than that which upon a million tongues has been briefly referred to as ''The Wakeford Case''.'

Horatio Bottomley, 1921

PART ONE

THE GIRL
IN THE CATHEDRAL

1
THE
ARCHDEACON'S STORY

It was a raw, wet evening. The train clattered away from Lincoln Station across a confusion of points and intersecting rails, past the silent iron mills and out across flat countryside still gaunt in the aftermath of winter. It steamed due east, following the placid River Witham; curving south-east in fading light to Bardney and Southrey, passing through Kirkstead and Dogdyke in rainy darkness, stopping at every station: then, straight as a die, south-west through Kirton and Algarkirk, like a glow-worm on a gigantic billiard table, moving across the dark fen landscape.

Cocooned in the bright warmth of a first class compartment the Archdeacon relaxed. It had been a busy day: the cathedral service at half-past ten, a sermon at quarter to twelve, the Bible class for the choir at three o'clock. His neat greying head rested on a GNR antimacassar, his sermon book and papers at his side on the chocolate-coloured upholstery. A punctual and punctilious man he would have noticed, with characteristic irritation, that the train was more than ten minutes late as it steamed into the gas-lit platform of Peterborough station at 7.50 p.m.

He probably left the station on foot, carrying his bag, for he still loved to walk, and within five minutes was striding up the three stone steps of a hotel in Westgate Street. The Bull Hotel was a curious choice for such a man. Despite its imposing eighteenth-century stone façade and an advertisement for the finest grill room in the Midlands (with 'first-class cuisine' and 'a unique cellar of wines at most modest prices'), it was a rough-and-ready commercial hotel. But the Archdeacon knew the place, he had stayed there before; it was close to the Cathedral where he had come — to be alone, to think, to seek inspiration for the sermons that he was to give in Liverpool later in the month. Even so, he was lucky to find a room, for by eight o'clock the inn was crowded with horse-dealers and breeders come from far and wide for the Horse Fair on the following day.

The proprietor of the Bull and his harassed wife had been coping with a large supper party in the hotel that evening; Seymour Hicks's theatrical troupe had completed its week's run with a farcical comedy called 'Broadway Jones' at the Hippodrome (Fred Karno's theatre in Peterborough) and the entire company had piled out of the hotel only minutes before the Archdeacon arrived. The plumbing had broken down under the strain.

There was only one vacant room in the Bull Hotel that night — Number 15 — a small room on the top floor with a single dormer window, overlooking Westgate Street and dominated by a large double bed, not at all suitable for a dignitary of the church. The Archdeacon said it would do, signed the hotel register and asked the proprietor, rather surprisingly, if there were many parsons staying at the hotel. He wanted 'quiet and solitude', he said, and did not want to be 'among a lot of parsons that were talking sermons'. With the Diocesan Conference coming on, the hotel would be a refuge from his colleagues, he explained.

The Archdeacon took supper by himself: a conspicuous figure in the gloomy dining-room, its walls hung with eighteenth-century portraits and yellowing prints. He drank half a bottle of claret and climbed the steep, narrow staircase to the bedroom under the eaves. He slept, as he said he always did, in a nightshirt.

The morning was wet and cold. The Archdeacon breakfasted at half past seven in the dining-room, went out to buy a newspaper and came back at ten past eight to read it in the grill room.

Just after nine o'clock, he crossed the lobby and went out again on to the narrow glistening pavement of Westgate, now busy with the Fair traffic, and smelling of horse dung and petrol fumes. By half past nine he was standing in St John's, the church in which his brother Onslow had been married forty years before. He spent some twenty minutes there. At a quarter past ten he was in the chilly Cathedral, the smell of damp stone in his nostrils. Matins had just finished. He settled down on a seat on the north side of the nave, near the west end, his sermon book on his knee, and started on the first of the five sermons that he had come to Peterborough to prepare. The cold was hard to bear and within an hour he was pacing about the great building trying to get warm, his footsteps echoing against the ancient stone.

At the west end of Peterborough Cathedral was a curious painting, set high up on the wall, to the right of the great doors. It showed an old, white-bearded man standing four-square with a spade in his right hand and a large bunch of keys in his left. Set in the wall beneath the picture was an engraved stone slab. Looking up at it, with a puzzled expression, was a girl in a wet raincoat, trying to read the archaic writing. She was about seventeen or eighteen years old the Archdeacon guessed. He deciphered the inscription for her and told her the man was Old Scarlett, a sexton who had lived to be ninety-eight and buried two famous queens. They walked back down the Cathedral together, Wakeford talking all the time in his strong, carefully modulated voice. At the entrance to the choir there were some railings and a gate.

15

Wakeford paid a shilling for them to go in, and showed her, on each side of the high altar, the burial places of Catherine of Aragon on the left and Mary Queen of Scots on the right.

His brief companion thanked him for his kindness and walked down the long nave to the west door of the Cathedral, watched by two vergers standing, black-clad and vigilant, in the chilly nave. The Archdeacon later chatted to one of them, crossed over to speak to the other (about the bad behaviour of visitors to the Cathedral) and then, hearing a man's voice echoing in public declamation, walked on to discover the Very Reverend Arnold Page, the Dean of Peterborough, testing the acoustics for his address to the forthcoming Diocesan Conference. They talked for a while and, with the morning gone, the Archdeacon made his way along the nave, passed beneath the memorial to the old sexton, and went out into the great porch at half past twelve.

The girl was still there, sheltering from the rain. They spoke again of Old Scarlett; the Archdeacon told her of a postcard of the memorial that could be bought nearby. Together, they went to the shop, where he had bought his newspaper that morning. The girl purchased a sepia picture of the old sexton and said goodbye a second time to the companion on whose account she was sought, within a year, throughout the Kingdom.

★　　★　　★

The Archdeacon lunched in the refreshment room at the Great Northern Railway Station. Then he went for a walk in the country, heading west along Thorpe Road, past terraced houses and villas, out into the bare countryside along a muddy footpath through Thorpe Park. By two o'clock he was nosing about inside a modest, stone church close by the roadside among the straggling thatched cottages of Longthorpe village. The caretaker, a local woman, was polishing the church brasses and they talked awhile. He admired the new reredos, the chancel screen and the lurid east window.

The Archdeacon left St Botolph's at a quarter to three and trudged down the steep slope of Sheep Wash Hill, from where he could glimpse the River Nene winding through flat pastureland — then on to the grey stone walls and houses of Castor. He was now five and a half miles from Peterborough — and extremely wet. At four o'clock he sought shelter in a thatched pub called the Fitzwilliam Arms. He took tea and gossiped with the landlord before braving the pelting rain to climb up to the cruciform church of St Kyneburgha, sitting neatly on top of a hill dotted with gravestones.

John Wakeford spent half an hour alone in the dim church, and at five o'clock headed back to Peterborough and the unsuspected dangers of the Bull Hotel.

He reached the Bull at around half past six. The hotel was in chaos again — full to the roof, the plumbing still out of order and the bar overflowing with damp, beer-swilling men from the Horse Fair. Jammed in among them, staring gloomily at the Hogarth prints on the walls, was a thin young man with a haggard elfin face who later became deeply embroiled in the Wakeford affair.

The Archdeacon marched in, soaking wet, and found there was no water for a hot bath. He had no change of clothing. He decided that he would eat straightaway and, after ordering a fire to be lit upstairs, squelched off to the dining-room only to discover that all the tables were occupied. He chatted with another guest while he waited, a conspicuous figure in his sodden clerical garb in a room full of farmers and horse dealers. One of them wondered whether the 'old parson' had come to Peterborough to buy a stallion.

He was given a table at seven o'clock, ate a hurried meal and climbed up to his little room under the eaves, to dry his clothes in front of the fire and retire early to the large double bed.

He appeared in the grill room at eight o'clock next morning. A young woman was drying her furs before the fire.

The Archdeacon ate his breakfast swiftly and, as on the previous day, walked out into Westgate and returned with a newspaper. He went over to the Post Office at half past nine to collect a letter which he had arranged that his wife should send there, and then walked to the bank where he cashed a cheque for two pounds. Back at the hotel he packed his bag, paid his bill (it came to about two pounds) and took the 11.0 a.m. train, via Boston — the way he had come — rather than the direct line north through Sleaford, for he wanted to deliver some parish council papers at Kirkstead. The familiar figure of Mr Lanyman, the parish clerk, would be waiting for him on the platform of the little station to collect them at 12.50 p.m. when the train stopped there.

The Archdeacon reached Lincoln at 1.33 p.m. and returned immediately to the Precentory where he lunched, with his wife, just after two o'clock.

★ ★ ★

Three weeks later on Good Friday 1920, John Wakeford returned to the Bull Hotel at Peterborough. He arrived at seven o'clock on an overcast April evening. He had posted a card in Chelsea, two days before, reserving a room.

He was desperately tired. All week he had been travelling and preaching. He had finished the services at Liverpool the previous Friday and had travelled back to Lincoln to give the Statutory Sermon in the Cathedral on Palm Sunday. The same afternoon he had gone, via Newark, to London and preached at St Luke's, Chelsea, in the evening. On each of the succeeding days he had preached once, or sometimes twice, and was now exhausted. That morning he had taken the Three Hour Service at St Luke's. But he had been summoned to Lincoln for a meeting with the Bishop, at eleven o'clock on Easter Saturday. To reach Lincoln that evening would have entailed leaving King's Cross at noon on Good Friday, so he had taken a later train and would catch an early one from Peterborough the next morning.

The Archdeacon signed the hotel register: 'J. Wakeford, Precincts, Lincoln'. He was probably talking as he did so, for the ink was already dry when he blotted the page.

There were only two other guests staying at the hotel and the Archdeacon was given a comfortable room, Number 5, to make up for the poky one with which he had had to be content during the Horse Fair.

The Archdeacon dined, half an hour after arrival, sitting in the empty public dining-room at the hotel. He drank half a bottle of claret and turned in for the night, greatly fatigued.

He rose early next morning. The hotel was scarcely awake when he appeared for breakfast, which was slow to arrive. With so few guests, breakfast was served in the private dining room. To save time, the Archdeacon asked for the bill to be brought to his table: it was for some twelve to fifteen shillings, he later recalled, and it was wrong. The mistake was put right and the Archdeacon gave the difference to the waitress.

He caught the 9.04 a.m. train from Peterborough, reached Lincoln by 10.40 a.m., and was met at the Great Northern Station by his son, Lieutenant John Wakeford, who was on Easter leave from the Royal Engineers. Father and son walked up the steep hill to the Precentory together. The Archdeacon looked over his mail and then went on to the Bishop's Palace — to discover that he was not expected and that there would be no meeting that day.

★　　★　　★

This was the Archdeacon's story of his visits to Peterborough: within a few months it captured the interests of millions of newspaper readers and was challenged in every important detail. The harmless-seeming events of March and April 1920 were twisted into an unrecognisable form by John Wakeford's enemies to leave a mystery that has never been satisfactorily resolved.

2
THE
TRAP IS SPRUNG

It was not until July that the crisis came. Mrs Wakeford received a peculiar message from her brother, who was a clergyman, asking her to meet him on the railway station at Burton-on-Trent. There, on the long draughty platform, Herbert Worthington asked his sister if she had stayed with her husband at the Bull Hotel, Peterborough, on the night of the 14th March? Evelyn Wakeford was astonished and replied that she had not. Worthington then told his sister that he was acting on behalf of the Bishop of Peterborough. If she had not slept at the Bull, then charges of immoral conduct would be brought against her husband, for evidence had been obtained that he had slept at the hotel with a woman.

In this way Evelyn Wakeford knew before her husband that he was to be brought to trial.

Worthington urged his sister to go back with him to the rectory at Netherseal and apply for a judicial separation from her husband; Evelyn Wakeford refused indignantly and returned to Lincoln. She told her husband what had happened and the next day, the 6th July, wrote to Worthington denying that she had slept at the hotel. Ten days later she went to Peterborough and was shown the register at the Bull.

On the 2nd November 1920 Herbert Worthington wrote to the Bishop of Lincoln.

Private and   Nether Seale Rectory
Confidential   Ashby-de-la-Zouch

My Lord Bishop,

I am sorry to trouble you with a very unpleasant matter. I enclose evidence delivered to me by a clergyman near here whose name I can give you. The Bishop of Peterborough knows all about this case also. As Mr Wakeford is my brother-in-law I don't want to appear in the matter, but I may say that I have every reason to believe this evidence. Your predecessor sent for me and wished to consult me how a scandal between J. Wakeford and a woman, whom Bishop Hicks named as Evelyn Porter, could be stopped. I would have nothing to do with the matter, but a month ago, or five weeks ago, I had a letter from some firm of lawyers in Leeds saying that if I did not come on the following Friday and make a full apology for the unfounded charges I had made against their client, John Wakeford, and sign it in such terms as they should then dictate, they would issue a writ against me for libel. I replied through my lawyers that I should not go to Leeds and should not withdraw anything, and they were ever welcome to issue any writ they liked. I have received none yet. My sister, Mrs Wakeford, for years — 17 or 18 anyhow — has told me the disgraceful way her husband has behaved, and my dear father, now gone from us, often discussed the matter with me. I leave the evidence in your Lordship's hands to deal with.

I am always yours very faithfully,

Herbert E. Worthington,
Rector of Seale and Rural Dean

NB — I hold my sister's letter, dated July 6th, to say she has not slept in Peterborough for three years.

The Bishop was reluctant to act. According to Wakeford he was forced into it by the Dean: 'When the accusation was made against me he hesitated and was disposed to veto the process, but he consulted Dr Fry, who vehemently demanded action'. Wakeford said that the Bishop was surprised by Fry's passion and spoke later of the Dean's bitterness in the matter. Nevertheless, Bishop Swayne gave the conduct of the case into the hands of the man whom Wakeford regarded as his enemy.

Wakeford responded in a letter written to the Bishop on November 20th, 1920.

> I have now had an opportunity of considering what course to adopt in reference to the most grave and baseless accusation brought against me by my brother-in-law, Mr Worthington. As they have been made to your Lordship by a clergyman of the Church of England I venture to hope that they might form the subject of an inquiry by the appropriate Ecclesiastical Court. I need scarcely add I shall be grateful if I am given the earliest opportunity of refuting the very serious and unfounded charges that have been made against me.

This request was granted. On the 20th December, the solicitors for the Bishop dispatched to Lincoln printed forms of complaint under the Clergy Discipline Act of 1892; on the 28th they were taken to the Bishop, together with Wakeford's reply. Copies were sent to the Chancellor of the Diocese, G.F. Talbot K.C. Assessors were needed to assist Talbot at the trial and in January three clerical and two lay assessors were selected by ballot. The clerical assessors were Archdeacon Jeudwine; Canon Akenhead, Vicar of St Martin's, Lincoln, who was well acquainted with Wakeford and the scandal which now surrounded him; and Canon Markham, Vicar of Grimsby, who was suspected by Wakeford of spreading malicious gossip about him. The lay assessors were a Mr F. Acton C.B.E., of Seacroft, and Dr Sprowse, of Spalding.

22

There was much activity in the Close as the trial approached. Application was made for Wakeford's solicitors to 'inspect and examine before the trial at an address in London all books, letters, documents and writing' which the prosecution intended using at the trial. Advice was sought as to the proper dress to be worn by the clerical assessors ('walking dress'); sketches were made to show how the Chancellor and assessors were to sit; instructions were given for 'a testament, ink (6 bottles), pens (8), and spare nibs, blotting paper, foolscap paper, book on clergy discipline, act and rules, statutes for 1889, a railway timetable' and a 'looking glass for the common chamber'.

★　　★　　★

The 4th February dawned cold and gusty. By ten o'clock the ancient stone Chapter House was packed. In the coloured light from the stained glass the Chancellor of the Diocese of Lincoln — clad in a black, lace-trimmed gown — sat with his assessors, three in cassocks and black academic gowns and two in morning-dress. Talbot, Chancellor of many dioceses, was a thin, severe-looking man with close-cropped hair, penetrating eyes and a cold manner. Edward Hansell, Chancellor of the Diocese of Oxford, opened for the prosecution.

'The case involves charges covering two periods, the first being from March 14th to 16th, and the second April 2nd, Good Friday, to April 3rd. The scene of the story is an hotel known as the Bull in Westgate, Peterborough, an hotel not frequented by clergy. Canon Wakeford asked the manager if it were so frequented and was told it was not.'

Mr Hansell said that the evidence was of two classes. The first would be given by five witnesses (Mr Pugh, formerly manager of the hotel, his wife, two servants and a friend of Pugh's) and the second by the police. 'It is a very remarkable circumstance that the evidence which will be given by the hotel witnesses is corroborated in no slight degree by the police.'

Hansell explained that the police had become involved because, shortly before, someone had been going about dressed in clerical clothes and passing worthless cheques. When they had learned that a clergyman had appeared with a woman at the Bull Hotel the police had 'naturally' wanted to see for themselves whether there was any connection with the previous frauds.

Counsel then related how the clergyman, 'who was wearing gaiters', had arrived at the hotel with a young woman and had been noticed by the hotel staff. The clergyman and his companion were shown to Room 15 ('a room which contained a double bed only') by a chambermaid, Mrs Willcocks. He had enquired about a bath and asked for a fire to be lit. While she was lighting the fire Mrs Willcocks heard Wakeford say to his companion: 'You must be very wise here. You must deny that you ever stayed with me.'

'After that, there was a very curious incident,' Mr Hansell continued, 'Canon Wakeford said he wanted a corner table in the [dining] room. That corner table was laid by Mrs Willcocks, who noticed that the woman had her hands on the corner of the table as she came to lay it. She heard the clergyman say, "Put your hands down, Mary." '

On the following morning the defendant had been seen by the Dean of Peterborough in Peterborough Cathedral, apparently showing a young lady around the building. He had signed the visitors' book.

Hansell recounted how the couple ('whoever they were') stayed at the Bull for another night and paid their bill after luncheon on Tuesday. The name in the register was 'J. Wakeford'. There were also the words 'Precincts, Lincoln' which had been added in pencil. After Wakeford's name the words 'and wife' had been added, also in pencil.

Counsel then turned to the second charge, covering the period 2nd to 3rd April. He said that a postcard had been received at the Bull Hotel asking for a double room to be reserved; the card was signed, 'J. Wakeford'. The couple had arrived on the afternoon of the 2nd April. They were alleged to have dined together and were seen in the hotel by Police Sergeant King and by a Mr Tuplin (a friend of the manager). Wakeford and his companion spent the night in the hotel and breakfasted together the following morning. 'Some communications' were later made to Canon Morse of Peterborough who inspected the register of the Bull Hotel and opined that 'the entry was in the hand writing of Canon Wakeford'.

Wakeford had later written to the Secretary of State for the Home Office. He had brought in the Chief Constable of Peterborough, who interviewed Mr Pugh and inspected the register of the Bull Hotel. There in the register was the signature 'J. Wakeford'. Underneath was another, 'M. Wakeford', allegedly added by the woman who was supposed to have spent the nights of the 14th and 15th March in Room 15 with the Archdeacon of Stow.

The first witness for the prosecution was Charles Pugh, formerly manager of the Bull Hotel. A dark man with a thin moustache, he described how on the 14th March a clergyman had walked into the Bull Hotel, between six and seven o'clock in the evening, in company with a woman, and had asked for a room. Pugh said that the hotel visitors' book contained the defendant's signature and he identified Wakeford in court. He was quite sure that there had been a pair of pyjamas and a lady's nightdress in Room 15.

Before Wakeford's second visit, Pugh had received a postcard, signed 'J. Wakeford', saying: 'Please reserve double-bedded room'. He confirmed that Sergeant King and his friend Mr Tuplin had been with him when he received Wakeford and his companion on the evening of the 2nd April. The hotel register had been signed 'J. Wakeford, Precincts, Lincoln' on this occasion, and Wakeford's companion had added 'M. Wakeford'. According to Pugh the woman was the same one who had accompanied Wakeford on his previous visit to the Bull.

The Dean of Peterborough confirmed that he had seen Wakeford in the Cathedral with a young woman. Although he did not wish to pledge himself to the exact date or time, the Dean was 'strongly of the opinion it would be on March 15th'. Then the rest of the Bull Hotel witnesses gave their evidence. Mrs Pugh described in a strong Scottish accent how a clergyman whom she recognised as Archdeacon Wakeford had stayed at the hotel with 'a lady about twenty-three or twenty-four years of age'. Fanny Willcocks, the chambermaid, affirmed that she had shown the couple to their room, where the gentleman told the woman to 'frankly deny' having stayed in the hotel with him. Willcocks had noticed that the woman was not wearing a wedding ring and seemed 'very timid'. At about mid-day on Monday, they returned to the hotel: the woman had handed her a parcel containing a nightdress and asked her to air it. Willcocks said that she had later been shown some photographs by a detective called Agar and had recognised them as of the gentleman who had stayed in the hotel with the young woman. She then identified Wakeford in the court.

When cross-examined by the defending counsel, Fanny Willcocks admitted that she had not recalled Wakeford's alleged remark about frankly denying the woman's presence until after the second of her three interviews with Detective Agar. 'It didn't cross my mind,' she said. 'It occurred to me that there was something wrong somewhere, but I let the matter go out of my mind.' When she was waiting at table, Willcocks added, the woman kept her hands down: it was then she heard the clergyman tell the woman that they would 'give the show away' by letting her hands be seen.

Another chambermaid at the Bull, Cissie Young, also identified Wakeford as the clergyman with the young lady. She said that she had seen a lady's nightdress and gentleman's pyjamas when she had taken hot water to their room.

Frank Tuplin, drapery manager of the Peterborough Cooperative Stores, said that he saw a gaitered clergyman with a lady in the Bull Hotel on 'the Sunday in March'. He did not speak to them. Some time later, when he was sitting in the private office of the hotel, he saw the couple again. Tuplin said that on this occasion Pugh had asked the lady to sign the register and she had done so.

The Chief Constable of Peterborough, Thomas Danby, next appeared to provide an explanation for the presence of the police officers who had been snooping around the Bull Hotel. Police Sergeant King, who had been in the hotel during both of Wakeford's visits, and a Police Constable Hall and Detective Constable Smith had also been watching the Archdeacon on the first occasion. Danby told how he had received a letter from the Home Office and had written to Wakeford, enclosing copies of statements which had been made by Hall and Smith after the Archdeacon's stay in March 1920. Danby said that he had been visited by Mrs Wakeford, who brought her husband's solicitor with her, and also by the Archdeacon himself who had told him that 'a very great mistake had been made'.

During cross-examination, the Chief Constable admitted that it had not occurred to him to ask Sergeant King for a report about his part in the events at the Bull Hotel. Certainly, if he had known that King was going to make allegations about Wakeford's second visit to the hotel, then he would have asked for one. According to the Chief Constable, police interest in the clerical gentleman was only 'in connection with cheques and was confined to March'.

The last witness to appear was Wakeford's brother-in-law. He said that he had 'heard of the Archdeacon being in Peterborough on March 15th and 16th' at a ruri-decanal meeting there in May. As a result of 'some conversation' at the meeting, Worthington had gone to the Bull Hotel and asked to see the register: he was shown an entry and recognised the handwriting of 'J. Wakeford', and of the address 'Precincts, Lincoln' as that of the Archdeacon of Stow. After 'consultation' with his Bishop, Worthington obtained statements from the Pughs and the hotel maids and these he forwarded to the Bishop of Lincoln. This concluded the day's proceedings.

★   ★   ★

The scandal of the Archdeacon of Stow was front page news in all the national newspapers next morning: 'ARCHDEACON OR AN IMPOSTOR?', 'DRAMA OF IDENTITY IN A CONSISTORY COURT', 'FAMOUS CHURCHMAN AND HIS HONOUR', 'ARCHDEACON ON TRIAL — ADULTERY CHARGES', 'ALLEGED HOTEL VISITS'.

The *Daily Express* made much of the drama of identity.

A distinguished-looking elderly man, dressed in the garb of an archdeacon and accompanied by a young woman, stayed at the Bull Hotel, Peterborough on two occasions in March and April last.

Was the clergyman Canon John Wakeford, Archdeacon of Stow and Precentor of Lincoln Cathedral, a man known personally to thousands, and, by repute, to scores of thousands, of churchmen throughout the length and breadth of the land, or was he an impostor for whom the police were searching?

This is the problem which must be decided by a Consistory Court at Lincoln, before whom Canon Wakeford appeared yesterday to answer grave charges of immorality.

★   ★   ★

John Wakeford gave evidence on the following day, relating how he had travelled to Peterborough on the 14th March and gone straight to the Bull Hotel from the railway station. There was no lady with him. He was alone. As there was a crush at the hotel because of the Horse Fair on the following day, he was forced to accept a double room. He wrote his name and address in the hotel register, had supper and went straight up to his room.

The next morning, at eight o'clock, he breakfasted in the public dining-room and then walked to the Cathedral where he made notes for his sermons. As he was about to leave, at around twenty minutes to twelve, he noticed a girl who was wet through and in 'a pitiable condition'. She appeared to be about seventeen years of age and struck him 'as being a pupil teacher'. He helped her decipher the memorial tablet and then walked with her along the nave: he was in no disguise and was dressed as he was in court. Later, he saw the girl again. She was standing in the cathedral porch and he took her to a stationer's shop and bought her a postcard. That was about quarter past twelve. He never saw the girl again.

When cross-examined, Wakeford said that he had not walked about the streets of Peterborough with a woman. He denied having gone to the Grand Hotel for a bath, as was claimed by the prosecution. Neither had he taken any meals in a private room in the hotel. On the Tuesday he had paid his bill to Mrs Pugh ('it was two pounds, more or less to within two shillings') and returned to Lincoln to take luncheon with his wife.

Wakeford rejected the evidence of the hotel staff. The register had not been brought to his room for signature as had been alleged. The statements of the Pughs and Fanny Willcocks were absolutely untrue; he knew nothing about the absence of a ring on the supposed lady's finger.

'There are eight witnesses who have spoken as to your presence with a lady on Sunday, Monday and Tuesday, including four hotel witnesses, and three policemen, with Mr Tuplin an independent witness. Have they been telling deliberate untruths?' Hansell demanded.

'Yes. As to the evidence of Mr Tuplin it is deliberately untrue that he saw me at the hotel with a lady. He has told a deliberate lie.'

29

'And is the evidence of the police also untrue?'

'Yes. They have made a mistake.'

'And did Mrs Pugh give false evidence and perjure herself?'

'Yes,' Wakeford replied rather enigmatically, 'I suggest that from the second week in March, from the 16th or 17th, there were Tuplin and King and Pugh all concerned to promote this case against me, and that the people of the inn — the satellites — were all concerned to bring this home upon me.'

Later, the questioning switched to the matter of meal charges — Wakeford's bill showed that he had been debited for meals for two persons on Saturday and Monday — before Prosecuting Counsel returned to his previous probings.

'Therefore, we have got eight people on the first visit who saw you there with a lady all of whom are untrue in this respect. Is it your suggestion that Mr Worthington is conspiring to ruin you?'

'Thank you for the opportunity...' Wakeford began to say, but Hansell interrupted him and said, 'Answer the question.'

'The late Bishop was approached by Mr Worthington with papers against me...'

'Will you answer the question,' the Chancellor interjected, 'yes or no?'

'Yes.'

'Is there any other conspirator?' Hansell asked.

'I know of none. There is another instrument,' Wakeford paused mysteriously, 'but he is a foolish person. He is used by them.'

Evelyn Wakeford was the last witness. She appeared briefly, telling how she met her brother in Burton-on-Trent and learned of the accusation that was to be made against her husband.

Mrs Wakeford told the court that she went to Peterborough on the 15th July and, again, on the 20th. On the first occasion she had been accompanied by a retired police superintendent called Theaker. Together, they went to the Bull Hotel where she heard for the first time of her husband's second visit on Good Friday. Mrs Wakeford examined the hotel register and had pointed out that 'some of the writing' had not been made by her husband. When she had asked Pugh how he knew who the supposed couple were, he had answered that 'they had been recognised'. After that, according to Mrs Wakeford, Pugh had 'gone sullen' and refused to say anything further. In conclusion, Mrs Wakeford maintained that her husband wore a nightshirt — not pyjamas, as had been claimed by the hotel witness.

It took the Chancellor of the Diocese of Lincoln and his five assessors an hour and twenty-five minutes to reach their verdict. The Chancellor announced it to the hushed assembly. 'We find the defendant guilty on each charge and that is the decision of us all, and I shall report to the Bishop, in pursuance of statute. The Archdeacon has the right of appeal to the Provincial Court.'

John Wakeford had been ruined by evidence that would not have been enough to hang a dog.

PART TWO

THE YEARS
OF PRIESTHOOD

3

DEVON AND SUSSEX

John Wakeford had always been a controversial figure: even in boyhood among the crowded streets and wharves of mid-Victorian Devonport.

The Wakeford family had moved from Kentish Town to the sprawling stone dockyard on the banks of the Tamar — called in Plymouth the Hamoaze — when John was eight. His father, William, was a policeman who had risen from the ranks to become Superintendent of R Division of the Metropolitan Police. In those days the Royal Dockyards were guarded by members of the Metropolitan Force and, at the end of 1867, John's father, an ambitious and masterful man, with his overworked wife and eight surviving children, was posted to supervise the policing of the Devonport naval yard. He had charge of more than sixty constables; on water as well as on land. The water police patrolled in long rowing boats and lived with their families on the hulk of a former fifth-rater, HMS *Leda*, built at Pembroke in 1828 and moored in the Hamoaze opposite the broken skyline of Vanbrugh's Gun Wharf. However, the Police Superintendent had a house just inside the dockyard gate in Fore Street, immediately to the right and close to the square-towered chapel. There were always policemen at the gate, but the Wakeford children could come and go as they pleased.

To a lively eight-year-old boy, the great dockyard was a magical place: forests of masts, cobwebbed with rigging, lined the straight stone quays; long teak hulls, some metal-clad, a few entirely of iron, and all with long bowsprits, creaked at their moorings; smoke drifted across the quays from tall thin funnels. John Wakeford, and his elder brother Robert, took to the docks and streets of Devonport like ducks to water and the busy Superintendent of Police and his overworked wife had little time to discover what they were up to.

According to John Wakeford's later account, he was not a scholarly boy. The schoolroom was close to the Superintendent's house, next to the police barracks and within earshot of the steam hammer shop. But the Wakeford boys, a pair of transplanted Cockney kids, lived in a world of smithies and mast houses and sail lofts and had no time for learning. They were tough and slovenly and despised milk sops. It would have been difficult to foresee a distinguished career in the Church for the unruly son of a dock police officer, but the two Wakeford boys caught the eye of a very remarkable man as they roamed the streets of Devonport. In Wakeford's own words, he 'tidied us up'. He not only made them wash, he taught them Hebrew.

It is difficult now to discern exactly what part the Devonport Rabbi played in the religious development of John Wakeford. Superintendent Wakeford seems not to have been particularly religious; Mrs Wakeford was devoutly low-church and it may have been her influence which led five of the children to devote their lives to the Church of England. But it was the kindly Devonport Rabbi whom Archdeacon Wakeford remembered years later with gratitude for setting him on the path to priesthood.

The first goal was matriculation and this he achieved in 1880, gaining a certificate from London University, it was

recorded, 'by private study'. This modest academic qualifi-
cation was, for the former dockyard ruffian, a considerable achievement and it served its purpose, because it was
deemed sufficient for 'John Wakeford of London University'
to commence training for the ministry.

★   ★   ★

John Wakeford set about his preparation with the help of the
Reverend Edward Read, Vicar of St Paul's in Morice
Square. Read had been at St Paul's for three years and the
young man was his first pupil. John was very well liked in the
parish. He had a fresh boyish face and intense penetrating
blue eyes; he showed great strength of character but his
devout manner was softened by kindliness.

He was summoned for examination in the spring of 1884.
After completing the formal written papers, candidates were
interviewed by the formidable Bishop Temple, who had
arrived at Exeter in 1869 amidst a storm of controversy over
Mr Gladstone's appointment of such a dangerous liberal. He
was described by an admirer as 'granite on fire' and did not
suffer fools gladly. The questions he set went straight to the
point, and no ordinand ever forgot his interview with him.
One candidate said that Temple's sledge-hammer blows had
battered him into a 'regular pulp of self-reproachfulness'.

But Wakeford, the outsider with only a hard-won London
Matric. to show against the B.A.s of the Oxford and
Cambridge candidates, came through the examinations with
flying colours. His strong personality appealed to Bishop
Temple, and he also caught the eye of the Examining
Chaplain for the Diocese, Alfred Earle, Archdeacon of
Totnes.

It was Earle who in 1885 offered the newly-ordained John
Wakeford a curacy in his own parish, at a salary of £150 per
annum. It was a thrilling prospect, and Wakeford knew
exactly how to go about his ministry. Nothing and no one

should be overlooked by the energetic young curate striding along the green lanes of West Alvington in the first glad consciousness of his priestly office. The parish covered four thousand acres, from great stretches of glistening estuarine mud to high breezy pastures with the smell of cattle and glorious sea views. It was a sprawling place; farmhouses and cottages lay scattered round the outskirts of the village. There was the big house at Combe Royal, too, with its parcel of ladies all anxious to meet the handsome young clergyman. At the slate-roofed village school in the shadow of the church tower were Mrs Goodman's young charges, dark-suited or in white pinafores, to be taught the Gospel story from the pages of *A Little Child's Guide to Jesus*. Above all it was Wakeford's impassioned sermons that filled the church and set the village maidens twittering.

His months at West Alvington were full of happy achievement; the good-natured Devon people responded to his enthusiasm and tolerated his autocratic ways. He was very handsome and had been sent by Parson Earle. Wakeford knew his popularity and his work flourished.

His imagination teemed with ideas. When his curacy ended, he planned to wander on foot, clad in cassock and belt, preaching in the fields, at village crosses and in parish churches. He imagined a brotherhood of missioners dedicated to a life of poverty, obedience and celibacy. It could be called the Order of St John and would spread throughout England, with six or seven brothers to every county. Their only sign would be a simple iron cross. They would bring the faith to the countryside in the way it had been brought to the coal mines and factories of the industrial north.

There was a snag, however. The Reverend Charles Atherton, recently installed as Diocesan Missioner, had definite views of his own on how rural missions should be conducted. Atherton was the first of the enemies that Wakeford acquired in his turbulent career. Formerly Rural Dean of Snaith in Yorkshire, he was a stubborn and pedantic man approaching fifty, experienced in mission work among the northern colliers. In Atherton's opinion 'it was of the *first* moment that we do not recommend any to our Missions, however good and holy they be unless they have been proved' — and young Mr Wakeford had not.

All the same, Archdeacon Earle managed to secure the Bishop's permission for his curate to become an evangelist — though unpaid, and licensed only for the Archdeaconry of Totnes.

Wakeford took to the road in March 1887, taking the style Rural Missioner. He headed north towards the villages on the north-eastern edge of Dartmoor. From Drewsteignton, with its tall church high up in the village with far views on all sides, he moved to Chagford and then on to Throwleigh, which backed on to the moor itself. He always entered the villages on foot, grave and impressive in his belted cassock, and stayed sometimes for a couple of days, sometimes for ten. As the spring advanced he was in the rolling country west of Okehampton. Here was real challenge, for there was evidently need of reform. The Rector of Northlew certainly thought so ('This place has been for many years notorious for its lawlessness and immorality'), and so did his neighbour at Bratten Clovelly ('a more disheartening place could not be conceived than Northlew'). The incumbent of Bridford was no happier, describing his parish as 'honeycombed with filth and malignant heresy'.

Wakeford took an uncompromising line, 'preaching plainly to the young men on the sin of bringing girls into trouble'. He not only denounced the sin itself but maintained in the strongest terms that marriage could not wash it out. No doubt to the anguish of many an anxious mother, and certainly to the surprise of one local squire, he condemned the practice of marriage in such cases as 'folly', arguing that 'true love cannot follow where respect is already gone'. He also waged a campaign against the danger of Non-Conformism, which was growing in Devon at that time. The churches filled quickly when John Wakeford preached. His sermons were violent and compelling.

To Archdeacon Earle, Wakeford's missions were remarkable, not least for their appearance of spontaneity: 'he goes to the most unprepared and neglected places without the long and, in many cases unpopular, preparation considered to be necessary in the ordinary formal mission'. But in reality they were planned with the exactitude and banal simplicity of a military operation — even paying regard to the lunar phase so that the inhabitants of outlying districts might walk back from meetings by moonlight. With his shining piety he transformed each mission into a glorious campaign for the risen Christ.

Each day there was an early celebration of Holy Communion, followed by a ten-minute address by Wakeford. At about a quarter past nine there were the school children to be instructed. Matins in the church was at eleven. At three o'clock there would be a service for women only, followed by Children's Evensong at a quarter past four. Sometimes there would be a service for the men of the village before Evensong, when, as well as a sermon, there would be 'doctrinal instruction'. The Missioner sought out the villagers in the fields and farmyards, or at home.

Wakeford stirred up the sleepy villages of mid-Devon all through the glorious summer of 1887. The Vicar of Chagford was delighted with the result: 'the impression Mr Wakeford leaves on all Parishes he has so far visited is *marvellous* . . . even Dissenters come, and in many cases have been brought back to the Church, through his able preaching.' The Rector of Throwleigh said his 'eloquence and earnestness and power of illustration are wonderful'. And the Vicar of South Tawton wrote, 'I never met with a priest who so strongly impressed me as a messenger of God.'

There was some hostility, however. The Rector of Kingsbridge told Archdeacon Earle that egotism was a conspicuous defect of Wakeford's character and there were

Bratton St. Mary,

(Commonly called Bratton Clovelly.)

A SHORT MISSION

Will be held in this Parish, APRIL 6th to 9th inclusive.

To the People of the Church and Parish of Bratton St. Mary, Clovelly.

At the invitation of him who has been sent by God to minister to your souls, and with the sanction of your Father in God, the Bishop of Exeter, we are about to conduct a Mission extending over five days in Eastertide, and commencing on the 6th day of April. A Mission is not for any one class alone; it is an effort to benefit for eternity the souls of all sorts and conditions of men. It is an attempt to reach Christ's sheep that are scattered abroad, that they may be saved by Him for ever; it has also a blessing of life more abundantly for those faithful ones who already know the Shepherd's voice.

And now we earnestly beseech you to prepare yourselves by self-examination and prayer for the setting forth of Jesus Christ crucified.

Pray without ceasing for a special Blessing on us all, that God's name may be hallowed, that God's kingdom may be strengthened and extended, and God's will be done on earth by men as in Heaven by the Holy Angels.

Grace be with you all,

Your servant for Christ's sake,

JOHN WAKEFORD.

Announcement for a Wakeford mission, 1887

other clergymen who did not want to have a young firebrand let loose in their parishes. The Archdeacon also discovered that Charles Atherton, the Diocesan Missioner, had started a whispering campaign in the Cathedral Close against the high-church upstart who was stealing his thunder in the Archdeaconry of Totnes. The Rector of Bridford wrote to Earle to warn him about it: 'I *know* — and I say this in confidence — that our Bishop's mind has been poisoned against Mr Wakeford.'

Here, for the first time, was a hint of the troubles that

dogged Wakeford for the rest of his life in the Church. His restless, passionate nature and his love of ritual and ceremony won admiration, reverence and, sometimes, love, but it also bred enmity and hatred of a kind that would eventually destroy him.

MISSIONARY - SUNDAY

"OH WE whose lives are lighted
With Wisdom from on High —"

Drawing by H.H. Munro (Saki)

Despite Atherton's influence, Wakeford continued his work in Devon. At the end of August 1887, he finished a mission at South Tawton, returned again to Chagford, moved on to Beaworthy, Belstone and Hennock and held a series of short services in Okehampton market place; these were interspersed with regular visits to Northlew, where the Rector, the Reverend John Worthington, was an outspoken ally. Wakeford's interest was not exclusively with the 'gross and shameless immorality' of the parishioners. Worthington's youngest daughter was a slim, dark-haired young woman with a handsome, oval face. For Evelyn Worthington, the arrival of the handsome young Missioner was a welcome addition to the dull social round at Northlew Rectory.

Opposition to Wakeford's controversial ministry was growing, however, as Atherton's malice worked its way through the Cathedral Close at Exeter. In desperation, Archdeacon Earle wrote to Bishop Bickersteth: 'If Mr Atherton and I act together and are kept in full cognisance of all that is going on, there need be no fear of clashing because I should know Mr Atherton's places and arrangements and he would know Mr Wakeford's through me. If this did not work then Wakeford should resign his licence at once, at five minutes notice, and get the Lord's work of a similar nature in another diocese.'

By January of the following year, Wakeford had had enough. Earle tried to make him stay. 'Do not decide about leaving the Exeter Diocese until we meet. I am giving very anxious thought to the work which is yours and mine.' But then another blow fell. Earle himself left the Diocese. Through the influence of *his* mentor, Bishop Temple, Alfred Earle was installed as a Suffragan Bishop in West London, and there he had his own problems for the London clergy objected, both as to the man appointed and to the manner of his appointment. In the midst of his own difficulties Earle wrote to fortify Wakeford against fresh troubles.

Kensington
March 18, 1888

My dear Mr Wakeford,

You need not trouble yourself at all about any reports such as that to which you refer. The cause was so very patent, if you had advertised in all the papers you could not have made the cause more clear. I cannot at all understand the position of the Rural Dean: he has always spoken so kindly and favourably of you.

Do not fear to trouble me with letters. If anyone wishes to write, let him do so: I will give my best attention to the matter. I am deeply sorry for the sake of the Diocese that you must leave it. I believe that your lines of work were those on which the most profitable work for the Diocese was to go forward. You will be terribly missed and no other work can quite fill the gap that will be caused. A very grave responsibility rests on the advisors of the Bishop, and on the Bishop also: it is a repetition of an old tale.

Always faithfully yours,

A. Earle (Bp. of Marlborough)

Let me know if I can do anything.

At this moment, when Wakeford was on the point of being driven from the villages of Devon, Bishop Earle sought the help of a powerful ally: a silver-haired, eighty-six-year-old man, with a strong Roman face, who was fitter and more athletic than many men half his age. Richard Durnford, Bishop of Chichester, was a brilliant classical scholar and a legend in the Church. He was an Alpine mountaineer, loved by small children and devoted to his walled garden in the Palace at Chichester. His pets included a pug dog, a headstrong Welsh carriage pony which he drove for upwards of twenty three years and a large Persian cat called Dare. This pampered creature he fed from the table with brown bread and asparagus stalks. It had a special chair in the study from which the Bishop would indignantly eject a visiting arch-deacon if he unknowingly sat on it.

Bishop Durnford was described as being 'as far removed from the North Pole of Dissenting Protestantism as he was from the Antipodes of Rome'. On the other hand, high-church practices flourished in his Diocese and his tolerant rule was thought by many low-churchmen to have led to the scandalous secession of some Brighton clergy to join the Church of Rome.

John Wakeford met Bishop Durnford at a Chichester Diocesan Conference. The thorny question of the appointment of Diocesan Missioner was to be considered and Bishop Durnford took the opportunity, when they had walked together in the gardens at Lancing, to discuss the matter with the man who was causing such a stir in Devon. Durnford was impressed, and announced to the Conference his intention of appointing a Diocesan Missioner. Alfred Earle's nominee seemed a natural choice and in October 1888 Wakeford was appointed Rural Missioner to the Diocese of Chichester.

★　　★　　★

John Wakeford prospered in the See of Chichester. He was almost as pampered as the Bishop's cat. Hardly a week passed without correspondence between the steely old prelate and the young Missioner roaming the Sussex villages. Wakeford was required to report regularly, not only on the villagers themselves but on the herons that were deserting their waters and going to Kent and on the great pike in Balcombe pond. The Bishop was a keen naturalist.

Occasionally, Durnford delivered a gentle rebuke or sent him a detailed criticism of the 'mission memorial cards' which Wakeford was handing out in extraordinary numbers to the Sussex peasants. But criticism was rare and invariably accompanied by unstinting praise for Wakeford's vigour and success in overcoming the 'heaviness' and 'solidified satisfaction' of the inhabitants of the Diocese of Chichester.

John Wakeford found time for authorship. In 1888 a slim, cardboard-covered volume appeared under the title *Rural Missioner*. Such is its confident authority that it is difficult to realise that it was written by one who had so newly entered the rural mission field. His second book was called *The Finding of the Cross*. It commences with Platonic simplicity 'The Truth is One, and all that is true coheres in one harmony', but swiftly qualifies the power of reason, 'the human mind is too narrow to embrace and human speech too meagre to express all the aspects of that Truth, which is the outspeech of the infinite Wisdom of God'. Then a direct mystical assault is developed on the Prince of Darkness himself, after briefly providing some insight into God's thinking about evil, 'If a time sequence in the Divine thought can be imagined the order doubtless is Evil foreseen, shrunk from, endured, conquered, destroyed.'

Wakeford wrote as he preached. His powerful imagination was packed with vibrant Old Testament imagery, poured out in staccato oratory, compulsive in its emphasis and repetition. Everything was made clear and certain. Evil was to be cut out and vices disembowelled. Christ's Kingdom must be carved out with the sword.

In the spring of 1891 Durnford sent his protégé off to meet Mr Gladstone. The Bishop had known Gladstone since 1827, when Durnford had been a tutor at Eton. Although not his pupil, Gladstone had sought Durnford's guidance as to his classical reading and had been told, 'Above all don't neglect Homer' — advice he obviously heeded. Durnford was also a close friend of Gladstone's brother-in-law, Sir Stephen Glynne, and it was Gladstone in the full power of his first administration who had recommended Durnford for the Bishopric of Chichester.

Durnford was anxious to hear every detail of Wakeford's visit to the Gladstones. He was well aware of the power that the fiery old statesman would wield in the Church if ever he returned to government, which he did the following year, at the age of eighty-two.

★   ★   ★

In the summer of 1893, John Wakeford was married. Evelyn Worthington had been attracted to the fierce young man during the first days of his Devon missions, but she must have felt there could be little hope of matrimony: Wakeford had no money and proclaimed the virtues of poverty and celibacy. But his dream changed and mellowed, and Evelyn grew to love him. The marriage was arranged and Wakeford accepted the offer of a curacy at Erdisley in Herefordshire.

The Worthingtons were an old Leicestershire family, related to the founders of the brewery at Burton-on-Trent. John Worthington, Evelyn's father, was a Brasenose man who had moved to Northlew eight years before from Farnworth in Lancashire, where he had been vicar for ten years. A genial, powerfully built man, he was well-liked in the village despite his adverse opinion of the parishioners. Millicent Worthington, the Rector's wife, was a small business-like woman with failing eyesight. Shrewd and assertive she did not share her husband's enthusiasm for John Wakeford.

Mrs Worthington's reservations were shared by Evelyn's elder brother. He had taken an instant dislike to Wakeford, who had so inexplicably won his father's respect and enthusiam. Herbert Edward Worthington was an elegant, snobbish man. Six feet four in height, and at thirty strikingly handsome, he had graduated from Merton College, Oxford, and after a curacy in Lincolnshire had been installed as Rector of Cadeby, Leicestershire (where he regularly hunted with the Atherstone Hounds): he was married to the daughter of the Venerable James Palmes D.D., Archdeacon of the East Riding of Yorkshire. Like the Worthingtons, the Palmes of Naburn were a prosperous family, with a regular sprinkling of clergy among the younger sons.

47

Evelyn Worthington had never been close to her brother, nor, it seems, had she ever really liked him. Herbert was the eldest of seven children — and she the youngest, and he treated her with contemptuous superiority. He liked to have his own way — even in the choice of his sister's husband — and had made up his mind that she should marry a close friend of his: the youngest son of the manor house at Ashbury, two miles across the fields from Northlew Rectory. Herbert Woollcombe was a tall, bearded, good-looking and amiable man. That Evelyn did not become engaged to him resulted more from Herbert Woollcombe's feelings on the matter than her own. They were on very friendly terms, but Woollcombe was haunted by the streak of madness which ran in his own family and which, he believed, had driven one kinsman to shoot himself and another to hang himself before breakfast. To Herbert Worthington's frustration, Woollcombe refused even to contemplate marriage and never proposed to Evelyn. Her choice of a penniless cleric, whose father had been a police sergeant, was more than her brother could bear.

Despite the forebodings of Mrs Worthington and the bitter disappointment of her son, John Wakeford's marriage was undoubtedly the social event of the decade in sleepy Northlew.

The 7th June 1893 dawned with lowering clouds covering the distant brown moors, mists clinging to the nearby hills. There was a choral Communion Service at eight o'clock at which Evelyn Worthington and John Wakeford took the sacrament. The church bells pealed intermittently through the morning, and by mid-day a strong wind had sprung up, clearing the mist.

By two o'clock the church was filled to overflowing. Most of the gentry from the surrounding districts were there, squeezed in amongst rows of white-surpliced clergy. Herbert Woollcombe was notable by his absence.

Evelyn Worthington wore a wreath of orange blossom

1 John Wakeford in middle age

2 *Left* Devonport, ca 1890

3 *Below left* Bishop Temple

4 *Below right* Bishop Bickersteth

5 *Right* The Rector of Northlew,
John Worthington, and his wife

6 *Below* Northlew Rectory

7 Bishop Durnford

veiled with tulle and a pearl and gold necklet. After the marriage, village girls strewed the carpeted path with flowers as John Wakeford led his wife to the comfortable stone rectory — and then to a honeymoon in Germany.

A few days later a letter from Bishop Durnford arrived at Northlew Rectory. It contained a telegram from Mr Gladstone announcing that the Prime Minister had laid Mr Wakeford's name before the Queen and that Her Majesty had approved his nomination to the living of St Margaret's, Anfield, in the Diocese of Liverpool.

Wakeford's visit to Gladstone two years earlier had not been in vain. The old statesman had remembered the young missioner from Sussex and when his first nominee (his own son-in-law) had hesitated, he offered the living of St Margaret's, Anfield, to John Wakeford: 'a clergyman as to whose qualities and services I possess such unequivocal testimony'.

4
LIVERPOOL

The vicarage of St Margaret's, Anfield, was an ungainly pile, built in the 1880s, with arched gothic windows and walls patterned with narrow bands of coloured bricks. It was a gloomy house and on winter days the gas had to be lit at three o'clock in the afternoon. There was no garden, only a solitary laburnum beside the front door. The gaunt, brick church and the school stood close by in the same plot of rough, sooty grass.

Dorothy Sheepshanks, the Vicar's four-year-old daughter, was playing with her younger brother before the fireplace in the drawing room when John Wakeford arrived. She knew that something very important was to happen; she had been told so, and her new clothes confirmed it. But she felt no special thrill at the thought of leaving home. The door clicked open, disturbing the children's play. Stooping down to them was a tall man in black, a gleam in his intense blue eyes. He said, 'You two are not going with the others, you know. You are to stay with me.'

The little girl remembered these horrifying words for the rest of her life. She was paralysed with fright: 'we were conscious that we disliked and feared this man. We said nothing at all, only gazed at him.'

Poor Wakeford's clumsy joke had been misunderstood. His impulsive charm had failed him for once, the children had read his face and been frightened by the inward intensity of his eyes.

Dorothy's father, the first incumbent, had come to the parish twenty years before. Anfield had then stood beyond the outskirts of Liverpool, with a population of only three and a half thousand and a scattering of large, prosperous houses. But by 1893 streets of back-to-back terraces had crept steadily across the open land and the neighbourhood had become poorer. The Workhouse was close by on Belmont Road, and the parish was now a rough, violent place. On pay days men got drunk and fights flared up in the streets, with fenders snatched from the fireside for weapons. The Vicar was sent for to restore order.

Like his successor, John Sheepshanks was a high-churchman. Confessions had been heard at St Margaret's; processions of chanting people carried banners around the huge, ugly nave. Such Popish practices of this sort attracted the venom of the extreme Protestant sects, especially on the 12th July when the Orangemen took to the streets. Mobs would arrive outside and stones flew through the vicarage windows, while the children cowered on the floor.

John Wakeford rose to the challenge of this poor, sprawling parish. Within days he was in the thick of things. His preaching was a revelation to the astonished parishioners, the deep, powerful voice filling the great church with the passionate certainty of the risen Christ. Eleven or twelve hundred would pack St Margaret's for the Sunday evening services and crowds were regularly turned away. The news spread through Liverpool of the astonishing revival. People came over on the Birkenhead Ferry. Local newspaper-men were dispatched to discover what was going on; even the *Liverpool Review*, not normally well disposed to high-

John Wakeford (cartoon from the *Liverpool Review*)

churchmen, sent along its reporter. He was overwhelmed: 'Mr Wakeford is a man of strong personality, both in the pulpit and out of it. In the pulpit, his intense vitality, his volcanic energy, his fire, his earnestness, his enthusiasm and perhaps his youth, take the heart of the listener by storm.'

At thirty-four, John Wakeford was tall and straight. He walked like a soldier, and there was an odd kind of boyishness about him. Away from the pulpit he had a quiet and deceptively nonchalant manner — at first sight he seemed almost unconcerned — and a manly good humour that pleased male and female parishioners alike. Yet in the confessional he probed their hearts and minds and, in the pulpit, burst forth in a passion of declamation.

These were not the only means that Wakeford used, however. In January 1894 there appeared the first issue of the *St Margaret's Review* (priced at one penny), a re-vamped version of John Sheepshanks's humble parish magazine. By the standards of the time, it was a very professional publication, with a blood red cover adorned with a bold black cross. There amidst advertisements for Jones's Venetian Dress Cloth (10½d per yard) and Macdonald's Highest Class Artificial Teeth (English and American Systems) John Wakeford let fly at the manifest evils of Liverpool society. In the first few months he took issue with the newspapers for 'the hurricane of misrepresentation and fiction blowing keenly about St Margaret's'; attacked the Unitarians for their woolly doctrines; castigated the Mayor of Liverpool for embracing that faith; and criticised the Bishop of Liverpool for consorting with the Mayor. The local parliamentary candidates were accused of fermenting sectarian riots, while Cardinal Vaughan was pummelled for the fallacies and superstitions of the Roman Catholics. There was a eulogy of Mr Gladstone on his retirement and a severe reprimand for the Walton Town Council for entrusting the care of the Anfield drains to a private company.

There were in fact few important local issues which did not

receive the attention of the Vicar. In January 1895 Wakeford
denounced from his pulpit the goings-on at the Liberal Junior
Reform Club *and* the Liverpool Conservative Club — they
were 'little better than drinking shops and gambling pits' —
and he was brought to court to apologise for his words.

The turbulent early years at Anfield were difficult for
Evelyn Wakeford. It could not have been an easy marriage;
she had been transplanted from lush, green Devon to a
squalid northern parish to find her masterful husband in a
constant turmoil of religious ardour and controversy. After
the peaceful social round of Northlew, Liverpool was a
depressing and fearsome place, scarred by poverty and
divided in religion; and its frontiers seemed to drive straight
through the Vicarage of St Margaret's. Her husband was spat
at by the loungers outside pubs; Protestant and Catholic
urchins alike shouted after the pupils of St Margaret's School.
And to make matters worse, John Wakeford was again at
odds with his Bishop, who was a dogged low-churchman.

Liverpool was an anomaly, in religion as in other things.
The furore surrounding the rise of Ritualism was subsiding in
England at the end of the nineteenth century, but not in
Liverpool. The struggle there intensified and was complicated
by politics. Wakeford was at the storm centre. His adversaries
were numerous and powerful, both within his Church and
outside it; where there were none he would create them.

A paunchy, lisping bachelor called George Wise was
particularly dangerous. This frock-coated and bespectacled
Cockney was born in Bermondsey in 1856, a collateral
descendant of the cobbler, John Pounds, who founded the
Ragged Schools. He had had a chequered career. Confirmed
in the Church of England, he had lapsed into scepticism,
recovered his faith and moved to Liverpool in 1888 to work
for the Y.M.C.A. and the Christian Evidence Society. There
he attacked Catholics and Anglo-Catholics with equal vigour.
His followers, known as the Wiseites, regularly demonstrated
outside St Margaret's, claiming that Ritualism had driven

G. W. Harris

George Wise (cartoon from the *Liverpool Daily Post & Mercury*)

working men from Wakeford's congregation. On Palm Sunday, 1899, Wise mounted an all-out crusade. He assembled his forces in Islington Square at a quarter to eight on a cold, rainy morning. They marched in a long, straggling procession with about seventy damp policemen plodding in file beside them. As they approached St Margaret's, Wise brought in reinforcements, including a drum and fife band; the procession now numbered several thousands.

The church was guarded by a line of policemen, who managed to prevent the Wiseites entering with the frightened worshippers, who scurried into the church, palm leaves concealed beneath their coats, to take part in a service with the enflaming Romanish title *Via Crucis*. Stones were thrown and police and sidesmen jostled, while the demonstrators blocked the surrounding streets hooting and jeering at 'Pope John of Anfield'.

This was only one of many such demonstrations. The *Liverpool Review* urged the Protestant Party to 'brawl on, and make these deaf and dotard bishops bring such high-churchmen to heel'.

Amidst all this uproar, Wakeford tended his ugly, divided parish with exemplary care and prodigious energy. No detail was overlooked, no misdemeanour too trivial to escape castigation. In addition to innumerable services, lectures, missions, Bible classes and outings, there was the renovation of the church to see to; new hangings for the east wall of the Chapel of the Resurrection; repair and improvement of the lectern; fund raising, for new 'very beautiful hangings' for the Sanctuary and for the cost of providing 'bouncers' at St Margaret's to evict 'irreverent intruders'.

John Wakeford was now greatly respected and genuinely liked in the parish. Men, women and children responded to the power of his preaching, the church was always packed for the Sunday services, where the people found colour and music and cadence that low-church and non-conformist services lacked. But for the Wiseites, St Margaret's was a running sore that must be cleansed, by fair means or foul, if not by the mob then by gossip and innuendo. For years, the lunatic fringe of Protestants had fed upon lurid stories of runaway monks and escaped nuns and the abuse of the confessional for the seduction of honest women; the handsome Vicar of St Margaret's was a prime target. An opportunity to besmirch him presented itself in the unlikely form of a Liverpool postman: William Wilson, a married man with three children.

Wilson had come to Wakeford's notice in February 1896 when he was ill with scarlet fever. Wakeford had organised a scheme for the care of the sick of the parish and, hearing of Wilson's illness, he visited the postman and later sent nursing sisters to the house. They came to him twice, on each occasion bringing 'only about a quarter of a pound of jelly', Wilson later recalled ungratefully. At the time, however, he had been much taken by Wakeford and, when recovered, he asked if he could attend the St Margaret's Bible Class, and also be prepared for confirmation. According to Wilson's later version of events, things came to a head one day when Wakeford took him to a side-chapel in St Margaret's and subjected him to a 'cross-examination'. He had said 'This is a confessional; I will not be confessed. I won't go on with the confirmation preparation, and will have nothing more to do with your church.' Wilson said that only then did he realise that he was intended to be the victim of a sinister Romanish practice.

William Wilson shook the dust of St Margaret's from his feet after this, but the trouble was that his wife did not. Much to her husband's displeasure, Mary Wilson continued to worship at Wakeford's church. This caused problems. The postman said that he returned from his duties at half-past eight one morning to find his children alone and unwashed, with no breakfast on the table. The same thing had happened when the children were ill with diphtheria. On another occasion, his wife had locked the children out of the house and one of them had been knocked down in the street by a drunken woman. These things were going on while Mrs Wilson was attending all possible events at St Margaret's, including early morning masses on Sundays *and* Wednesdays, as well as keeping up with the Church Literary Society and the Ward of St Albans. Worse, she had become the part-time housekeeper of Mr Eddrup, the unmarried Curate of St Margaret's; she had been seen leaving his house as late as ten o'clock at night and was once supposed to have spent the night there.

The postman poured out his troubles to packed meetings of the British Protestant Union and in subsequent divorce court proceedings, when he alleged that his marriage had been ruined largely as a result of interference in his life by the clergy of St Margaret's.

For two years the Wiseites smeared St Margaret's with stories of the postman's wife and shouted about priests' harlots and their bastards. Wakeford eventually lost patience and replied in the church magazine. He did not mince his words: Wilson was a wife-beater, a man 'who had treated his wife with sullen brutality'. How could St Margaret's 'have spoiled the happiness of a home that was never happy?' Nor could it be 'charged with quarrels that began six years before either Wilson or his wife had anything to do with our church'. Wilson was merely a paid 'dupe' of the British Protestant Union who could be relied upon to supply 'occasional fiction' when required.

Three months later Wakeford was sued for libel and all Liverpool learned of the scandal.

At the action in the Liverpool Court of Passage, Wakeford and his counsel firmly denied that Mrs Wilson had been improperly influenced by the St Margaret's clergy. Wakeford said he had met her only once, and, despite her assertion to the court that she would follow Mr Eddrup *anywhere* ('even into the Salvation Army'), he was convinced that no impropriety had occurred between his Curate and Mrs

Wilson. As to the alleged libel, he wrote what he did 'for an express purpose deliberately thought over' and was convinced of the necessity and justification for so doing.

The court found Wakeford guilty. He was ordered to pay damages of £150, and costs, to William Wilson. It was a dreadful verdict for Wakeford. The point at issue had been only his libel of Wilson, but the court hearing had played into the hands of George Wise and the British Protestant Union. Wakeford had seen Mrs Wilson only once; even Wilson had testified that *he* did not believe that the St Margaret's Curate had seduced his wife.

The *Liverpool Review* had a field day with Wakeford's defeat: a wife had been 'distracted from her domestic duties by the fascinating system of worship in vogue at St Margaret's,' it said. 'It is notorious that this is a common effect of the ritualistic system of worship; weak feminine minds are readily led astray by theatricalism. The ruined home of the wife who has been led astray does not enter into their calculations,' the article went on. 'There can be no room in the Church of England for a practice which has been proved by bitter experience to be a cruel and insidious instrument of moral and material destruction — a wheedling enemy to domestic confidence and virtue, a snuffling canting peeper into the sanctities of family life. This is the lesson of the Wakeford Case: ritualism is not British — it must go.'

There was little that Wakeford could do to disperse the miasma of gossip that surrounded St Margaret's, but he fought back, labelling the anti-ritualist crusaders a 'low mob of ruffians'. He spoke out against the Church Discipline Bill — another piece of Protestant devilry — that had been largely concocted in Liverpool by Austin Taylor's Churchmen's Council and Laymen's League, with the vigorous support of George Wise and a rising young Liverpool lawyer and politician, F.E. Smith. The bill aimed to banish the confessional and the mass by abolishing the episcopal veto and depriving ritualistic clergymen of their livings.

Wakeford had criticised the bill in detail in the *St Margaret's Review*, in the pulpit and at a public meeting in London. The *Liverpool Review* called him a 'goose' and a 'clerical swashbuckler' and his 'vilely slanderous' attacks 'a farrago of nonsense': he picked up mud from the gutters and wallowed in it. Worst of all, he was a coward who concocted slanders in Liverpool and fled to London to utter them.

John Wakeford battled on through the summer of 1903. George Wise was also fully engaged, for he had acquired a powerful rival, John Kensit, who had already achieved national notoriety as the formidable leader of the Kensitites, causing upheavals in ritualist churches throughout the land. A rabble rouser and former draper's assistant, Kensit was a prolific writer of evangelical tracts which he published from a shop in Paternoster Row, in the windows of which he displayed such fearful Popish objects as scourges, hair-shirts and penitential lashes. He had arrived in Liverpool with his son in the spring of 1902 to organise a crusade. He unleashed Protestant mobs against Catholics and high-church Anglicans alike. George Wise, not to be outdone, recruited a dangerous man called Arthur Trew, who had lately served a prison sentence for inciting riots in Belfast. In September 1902, Wise and Trew led a mob of Orangemen into battle with Irish Catholics in the Seaforth district; in October, John Kensit was struck with an iron file in a fight at the Birkenhead Ferry and died several days later.

George Wise was himself in trouble with the magistrates at this time. He was found guilty of obstruction, of holding a meeting outside John Wakeford's church and, later, of lewd behaviour in his public assertions that the priests lived with whores and robbed the poor to feed their bastards. Wise was defended by F.E. Smith, who was to play a decisive role in Wakeford's life. Smith also argued Wise's appeal in the King's Bench Division. He lost the case; not that he minded, for the Lord Chief Justice wrote to congratulate 'F.E.' on his conduct of it. Smith had the letter framed and hung it in his

60

chambers. Wise was left with the alternative of ceasing his open-air meetings or of going to gaol for two months. He shrewdly chose the latter. After a final 'monster indignation meeting', Wise presented himself — a wronged Protestant martyr — at Walton Gaol. He arrived in an open carriage; was allowed to wear his normal clothes, kept his books and papers about him; ate specially cooked food sent in from outside; and graciously received the Lord Mayor and Lady Mayoress who arrived bearing huge bunches of flowers.

Wise's imprisonment caused fresh violence on the Liverpool streets, and so did his release in June 1903, when 60,000 supporters followed him from prison to St Domingo Pit (an unenclosed space where several roads met next to a recreation ground) which had become the Wiseites' open-air forum.

John Wakeford was not intimidated. He continued to hurl defiance from the pulpit, and in the pages of the *St Margaret's Review*, at Protestants and Catholics alike. But conflict was only a small part of his life. In the worrying times at the turn of the century, when there was war in South Africa and trouble on the streets and in the churches of Liverpool, he was deeply involved in the Church School and was respected and liked by the stern, walrus-moustached headmaster, Frank Brummitt. At Wakeford's instigation, a Boys' Brigade troop was formed; ninety boys joined and met every Monday night for drill and games. A magic lantern was purchased to enliven geography lessons; part-time staff were appointed for evening classes in French and violin-playing; instruction was even arranged for the girls in typewriting.

Wakeford was good with children. He never talked down to them and, unlike young Dorothy Sheepshanks, they generally responded to his genial, boisterous advances. His son remembers him as an excellent companion. However hard the day had been, his father would be waiting in his study (which he shared with a large rabbit called Peter) to take down a book from the shelf and read a bedtime story to his

61

son. The young John Wakeford was a sickly boy and, on medical advice, was regularly packed off to his grandparents to get some fresh Devon air into his lungs. The boy loved his holidays at Northlew, although he sometimes felt the enmity which his uncle bore his father. Herbert Worthington's daughter — born at the same time as Wakeford's son — was physically and mentally handicapped and it was more than Worthington could bear to see Wakeford's child active and enjoying himself. If the boy came into a room, his uncle would walk out.

Young John, then six years old, spent the summer of 1904 at Northlew. It marked a turning point in his life, for his health began to improve. Later on, in Liverpool, father and son would bicycle together for miles through the surrounding countryside, usually towards Chester or Tarporley. Twice they explored the rolling green country of the Welsh border and the castles which Wakeford brought vividly to life for the boy. Once they went to France and bicycled through the unspoilt valley of the Loire.

Father and son were boon companions, but it was John's sister, Kathy, who was Wakeford's especial pride. She was a lively, brainy girl, three years older than her brother, and Wakeford had high hopes for his schoolgirl genius. Fortunately, young John — generally referred to as 'Kathy's brother' — regarded this with good humoured resignation.

Despite his popularity in the parish, Wakeford had only a few close friends in Liverpool: none were clerics. One was the local pharmacist, another a teacher of music. Wakeford was also on friendly terms with some of the doctors at the Workhouse Hospital on Brownlow Hill, and on Saturday evenings they would push back the surgical equipment and engage in vigorous boxing bouts under the harsh lights of the operating theatre.

In the shabby streets, gossip and innuendo continued, all centred on the affair of the postman's wife, and were obscenely embroidered by Pastor Wise and his congregation.

Wakeford's chance to clear his name came not in Liverpool but in the south. The *Southend Echo* had published a series of articles and letters on the iniquities of ritualism in the Church of England and particularly the immorality of the confessional. One of the letters referred to the now legendary escapades of the Anfield postman's wife, movingly depicting the plight of her husband: forced to wash, dress and cook for their neglected children, while his wife 'stealthily attended ritualist services against his known wishes — and even threatened his life.' According to the *Southend Echo*, it was a vivid example of the evils of the confessional in 'lowering the moral ideals of a nation', dangerously threatening the 'moral character of both penitents and priests'. The writer could provide names and dates of the provincial newspapers in which all the sordid events were detailed.

Wakeford brought a libel action against the Southend Borough Printing Company, and its proprietor, Mr P.E. Barnes. The jury decided that there had been libel and awarded Wakeford forty shillings damages.

Technically, Wakeford had cleared his name and exulted about it in the next issue of the *St Margaret's Review*; but the unjust stain of a priestly womaniser would remain; his enemies saw to that.

★   ★   ★

By 1906, Wakeford was no longer at the centre of religious strife in Liverpool. The direction of the battle was changing; it had now developed into a bitter struggle between Catholics and Protestants alone

This period was a watershed in Wakeford's life. At forty-six years of age he was establishing a national reputation as a preacher, author and man of affairs in the Church. When Edward VII died in May 1910, Wakeford preached at an open-air Memorial Service in Sefton Park to a crowd of 20,000 — the largest congregation one man had ever

addressed, according to the *Liverpool Daily Post*. His admirers
in Anfield were convinced that he would soon be offered a
canonry or an archdeaconry, if not a bishopric; but they were
wrong. Wakeford was not called. The attention of the Prime
Minister, H.H. Asquith, was indeed drawn to Wakeford as a
possible successor to the scholarly and well-connected Canon
Scott-Holland at St Paul's Cathedral. Asquith sought the
advice of the Archbishop of Canterbury and the Bishop of
Liverpool. The Archbishop was guarded. 'All I know of
Wakeford (it is not, as I have said, very detailed) is to the
good.' But the Bishop of Liverpool had Wakeford's measure.
'The appointment of the Rev. John Wakeford as a Canon of
St Paul's Cathedral would certainly be justified by his
excellence as a preacher. There are few men in the north of
England who are equally attractive in the pulpit.' However
the Bishop had doubts, 'I hesitate to recommend him as the
successor of Canon Scott-Holland. He still, occasionally, says
and does things that pain his friends and give a handle to his
opponents. He is a little difficult to work with and has to learn
to appreciate those who differ from him and to restrain a
tendency to self-assertiveness, and to impulsive speech and
action.' In the Bishop's opinion, a 'lesser canonry' would be
more appropriate.

Thus, unknown to himself, John Wakeford was passed
over for high office. A lesser opportunity presented itself when
the Lord Bishop of Lincoln, Edward Lee Hicks, wanted the
Vicar of St Margaret's to fill a prebendal stall at Lincoln: this
was a non-residential office, which carried the obligation
occasionally to preach and minister in the Cathedral. Hicks
had the reputation of being a keen radical. He had been
enthroned at Lincoln in the summer of 1910 and this was the
first appointment he had made. Wakeford was duly installed
as Prebendary and Honorary Canon at Lincoln Cathedral
on Friday, 23rd December 1910.

★   ★   ★

8 The Wakefords at Anfield
Vicarage, ca 1896

9 St Margaret's, Anfield

10 Lincoln Cathedral: west front and minster gate, 1920

11 Dean Fry

12 John and Evelyn
Wakeford in the
Precentory garden
at Lincoln

13 Sub-Dean Leeke
(right) at Lincoln,
ca 1911

In May 1912, the Precentor of Lincoln and Archdeacon of Stow, the Venerable John Bond, died. Bishop Hicks swiftly appointed an old Oxford friend to the vacant archdeaconry. The precentorship, and a residentiary canonry, were offered to John Wakeford and the offer was accepted.

The Liverpool newspapers were cock-a-hoop. Here was recognition at last for the man they now described as an 'able organiser, brilliant extempore preacher and orator, and one of the finest teachers in the Anglican Church'. All the unpleasantness of earlier years was forgotten. The *Liverpool Echo* said that Wakeford's 'rise in the Church was but a fulfilment of the predictions indulged in by those who knew him best in this city'. The *Liverpool Daily Post*, impressed by the value of the appointment (£1,200 a year), concluded that Wakeford's success resulted from 'a sound constitution, abstinence from liquors (spiritous and malt) and from any form of tobacco, and a delight in the discharge of what he feels to be his duty.'

Prebendary Wakeford was installed in his new offices on the 14th June 1912. One hundred and seventy parishioners made the journey to Lincoln for the installation, in special coaches on the train, all labelled 'St Margaret's, Anfield'.

Wakeford returned to Anfield and took his final leave of St Margaret's in August. The huge church was packed and many people were turned away. A collection was made for a commemorative tablet to record Wakeford's years in the parish. In his last issue of the *St Margaret's Review* he published a reading list for the more scholarly of his parishioners to pursue after his departure. They were to study church history, systematic theology and devotional theology as well as Illingworth's *The Catholic Atlas*, *The Doctrine of the Trinity* and Mortimer's *Catholic Faith and Practice*. He was long remembered in his shabby parish, and the eyes of old ladies still shine at the memory of him.

5
LINCOLN

The contrast between Anfield and the Cathedral Close at Lincoln was sharp and complete. In the great building, planned by the Norman Bishop Remigius and completed by St Hugh and his successors, John Wakeford's destiny was to be worked out.

To climb the steep, cobbled streets to the precincts and the houses round the Exchequer Gate is an exhilarating experience. There is a sense of being high up, but enclosed, with strong clear light and a fresh, almost maritime, movement of air among the cluster of ancient buildings.

The Wakefords arrived in Lincoln on young John's fourteenth birthday. Their daughter Kathy, now a striking-looking girl, was seventeen and still, in her father's eyes, a brilliant scholar; she was going up to Cambridge the following year.

For Evelyn Wakeford the move to Lincoln meant a comfortable home for her family at last, in the old stone Precentory in a corner of the Minster Yard, with a view of the great round arches of the west front. Behind this large house was a pleasant walled garden that was to become her special joy, and she soon wanted a bricked-up window opened, the better to glimpse the Precentory flowers.

Wakeford was now a prominent figure in the sheltered world of the Cathedral Close. As Precentor, he was second only to the Dean, taking precedence over the other residentiary canons: the Chancellor, the Sub-Dean and an Archdeacon, who was fourth canon. As a high-churchman, of colourful tastes, with little experience of cathedral life and only a recently acquired Durham Bachelor of Divinity (without examination) to cover up his London 'Matric', he was an oddity in the conservative Lincoln of 1912. Wakeford's fellow canons had impressive family connections, degrees from Oxford and Cambridge and College Fellowships.

The Dean, the Very Reverend Thomas Fry D.D., a Scholar of Pembroke College, Cambridge, had arrived at Lincoln three years before. Fry was a fierce little man with a round bald head and a bushy white beard, who had recently been headmaster of Berkhamsted School where he had been a notorious flogger. In his scarlet doctor's robes he looked like a miniature and rather cross Father Christmas. He was acutely aware of his small stature and retained the brisk autocratic manner of a Victorian pedagogue. The novelist Graham Greene was distantly related to Fry and knew him when his father was a housemaster at Berkhamsted. Greene thought him a sadistic brute.

Dean Fry was disliked by the cathedral staff. The lay clerks resented the fact that he rarely acknowledged their existence. Twice a day Fry would march past them as they waited respectfully outside their vestry. They would stand and bow to him, but he would invariably pass by, his eyes firmly to the front. His manner at meetings of the Chapter was thought cold and sneering. Yet he could be charming if the occasion demanded it; the Anfield parishioners, when they were in Lincoln for Wakeford's induction, were thrilled at his courteous reception of them at tea after the ceremony. His Bible classes for men, which were held in the Deanery on

Sunday afternoons, were popular and well-attended. A ticket collector at Lincoln railway station was a particular admirer ('The Dean on Sunday afternoons, my word, he's a grand old gentleman, he explains it all, it's my week's joy, is that time on Sunday afternoons.').

Fry was married to a woman like a bossy pouter pigeon. Julia Fry kept a parrot in a cage in the front hall of the Deanery. The bird perhaps hinted at the true relationship between the Dean and his wife when it said to a visiting Assize Court Judge: 'Julia, you old devil, shut up!'

Wakeford's immediate subordinate in the cathedral hierarchy was another small man, Canon Crowfoot. A sweet-natured man, his tiny figure was quite swallowed up in the enormous cathedral pulpit, but his sermons, delivered in a clear, fine voice, were perfect in phrasing and wonderfully uplifting.

The third residentiary canon — the Sub-Dean — was thought eccentric. Canon Leeke was a brilliant scholar, a Second Wrangler of Trinity College, Cambridge, and an enthusiastic bicyclist. He could be seen at all hours of the day and night pedalling around the Minster Yard or careering down the steep cobbled streets, his frockcoat flapping, taking food to the houses of the poor. He was much loved for his infectious laugh, his generosity and his concern for the aged. He was a man of firm convictions and a force to be reckoned with at Chapter meetings. He was also unpredictable, independent and remorseless, arguing a case against any opposition. His father, before he had been ordained, had been an ensign in the Oxford and Bucks Light Infantry and carried the regimental colours at Waterloo.

The fourth residentiary canon, and Archdeacon of Lincoln, was the ninety-year-old William John Kaye. He was a Balliol man, the son of a bishop who had married a bishop's daughter. Archdeacon Kaye was an extreme Protestant and made it his business to protest about any high-church intrusions that came to his notice. He was usually in profound disagreement with his brethren of the Chapter on almost every issue. When one of the four weather vanes on the pinnacles of the central tower stuck and could not be made to move in synchrony with the other three, the cathedral wits likened this to the Chapter in conclave.

Archdeacon Kaye lived for nine months of the year at Riseholm Rectory, a few miles north of Lincoln. His migrations to and from the precincts were notable features of the cathedral year. The Archdeacon's chattels were piled high on a horse-drawn dray and were invariably topped by an ancient hip bath. He walked with a slow stork-like gait, and performed his duties punctiliously when he was in residence. Kaye was the last of the residentiary canons to continue the custom of preaching a sermon from the nave at three o'clock on a Sunday afternoon. He once attempted to battle his way to preach in the Cathedral in the teeth of a ferocious snow storm and got stuck in a snow-drift. He was spotted by an aged cathedral constable who attempted to rescue him; both men sank in the snow until pulled out by some passers-by.

As Precentor, Wakeford had special responsibility for the choir. The cathedral organist, Dr Bennett, was a thick-set, humorous man with a walrus moustache. On Sunday mornings, he would arrive at the Cathedral in top hat, morning-coat and spats, carrying a rolled umbrella. He was prone to ungovernable rages, and had been known to burst from the organ loft in the middle of a service to drag a choir boy away by the ear for chastisement. Boys who did not open their mouths wide enough when singing had Dr Bennett's tobacco-stained knuckles forced between their teeth. He was perpetually at war with one or other of the cathedral staff. For years he was at odds with Dean Fry and the two men never spoke to each other, communicating only by formal letter. Eventually Dr Bennett apologised: 'Mr Dean, I admit that I backed the wrong horse.' But their relations remained frosty and Bennett would sometimes remark from the organ loft that Dr Fry had the voice of a cock sparrow.

John Wakeford swept into this odd little community and transformed it. The Bishop was determined that the new Precentor should carry all before him in matters of reform and organisation, even warning Dean Fry to give Wakeford a free hand.

The changes Wakeford made were radical and extreme. Choral Eucharist was introduced and celebrated every Sunday and on Saints' Days. Matins was separated off from these new services and the statutory sermon was preached in the morning at Choral Eucharist. This experiment was not entirely to Wakeford's liking and the sermon was put back to Matins and a second sermon, preached by a member of the Chapter, was inserted into the Eucharist. The Litany and Anthem in the nave were abolished; Choral Evensong was revived in the choir on Sunday afternoons and copes were to be worn by the three ministering clergy in the sanctuary.

Surprisingly, in view of all these drastic alterations, Wakeford got on famously with the formidable Dr Bennett. The Precentor's knowledge of cathedral music was rudimentary and, characteristically, he would develop sudden and unusual whims about what should and should not be played in the services. But Bennett managed to keep these in check and the two men developed an amicable relationship.

Wakeford's high-church innovations were judged and scrutinised by the cathedral folk as autumn gave way to the cold winter of 1912: by the choir-boys in their Eton suits and the priest-vicars in morning-dress; by Archdeacon Kaye, in his black university gown, perched uncomfortably next to Wakeford in his fourteenth-century stall, and hating the new-fangled goings-on; by Dr Bennett in the organ loft, and by the rows of doctors, lawyers, tradesmen and retired army and navy officers shivering, top hats on their knees, with their wives and daughters in Sunday finery packed in the remaining choir stalls or in the body of the Cathedral.

It is a testimony to Wakeford's powers of persuasion that he was able so swiftly to mould the new services to his design,

for the Cathedral Chapter were a contentious bunch. Much
bad feeling had been generated the year before by Dean Fry's
summary dismissal of the Senior Verger. The Chancellor, the
Sub-Dean and the Archdeacon had all protested at the
unfairness and harshness of Fry's action, but to no avail; the
fiery little Dean got his way.

★　　★　　★

Archdeacon Kaye died the following year. In his place George
Jeudwine, then Archdeacon of Stow in the Diocese, was
appointed to the fourth canonry as Archdeacon of Lincoln.
Bishop Hicks gave the Archdeaconry of Stow to John
Wakeford to add to his precentorship.

Beneath a large beard and rather cold manner, Archdeacon
Jeudwine concealed a friendly and sensitive nature, but he
had no time for intrigue or gossip and proved to be a
formidable antagonist at the increasingly stormy Chapter
meetings. When Fry attempted to bully him, Jeudwine
replied simply, 'Mr Dean, you behave like a baby.' Fry
jumped up and left the room. Jeudwine said, 'Now I think we
might go home to lunch.' But the Dean did not give up so
easily.

When Wakeford issued an order that the cathedral doors
should be locked at the commencement of services, Fry seized
on the unpopularity of the edict and countermanded it. It was
a habit among older worshippers to slip into the Cathedral by
the north door on Sunday mornings, towards the end of the
service, to take communion. Most of them were infirm and
found it difficult to sit through the whole service. Wakeford
had already got into a public row with one such miscreant
who was attempting to leave and the congregation was not
edified. Letters of complaint were sent to the Dean; Fry leapt
at the chance of scoring off Wakeford and thereafter the doors
were left unlocked.

In the matter of the Cathedral Choir School, Wakeford

won the day. This was a boarding school with a fine reputation, modestly housed some three hundred yards to the north of the cathedral, in Northgate. The schoolroom was in a small building just round the corner in Nettleham Road. Wakeford was determined to move the school to the Burghersh Chantry, an attractive eighteenth-century house with a squat Doric porch in James Street, off Eastgate. Sub-Dean Leeke was convinced that the scheme would be ruinously expensive and passionately opposed it. But Wakeford carried the Chapter with him and the removal took place. As things turned out, it was a financial disaster: the school was soon forced to close and the great choral tradition of Lincoln suffered an irreparable loss.

Another area of conflict was the cathedral library — the long, elegant room above the north range of the cloisters, designed by Christopher Wren, and the Wickham Annexe containing amongst others the books presented to the Dean and Chapter of Lincoln by Dean Honywood in the seventeenth century. The library was in considerable disorder and it was feared that many of the volumes had been stolen. Dean Fry had, in fact, produced a list of two hundred and fifty-nine missing items which he had circulated to the police and to the second-hand book trade.

The Chapter elected Wakeford to the librarianship and he took vigorous steps to reorganise the library. He engaged an expert, a Dr Buchanan of Chelsea, to help him sort the books. Two hundred and fifty-one of the missing volumes were found to be still in the library; only eight were lost. When Fry was informed of the discovery of the missing books he refused to believe Wakeford, nor was he prepared to go to the library to look for himself. According to Wakeford, the Dean expressly forbade any public announcement of the discovery of the lost volumes.

By the end of 1913, a strong antipathy had grown up between the Precentor and the Dean. Wakeford detested Fry's methods, not only his overbearing public attitudes, but, even more, what Wakeford considered to be his underhand dealings. Wakeford was shocked at being taken on one side and warned that a vote against a particular candidate for tenancy of the Chapter lands would be regarded by Dr Fry as a personal affront. He looked on him as a sinister figure, and recalled years later how Fry had boasted of his devious methods. At a League of Purity meeting he told how in Dorset in 1886 Fry had employed a detective to watch one of his parishioners and when he had acquired sufficient damning information 'the man was removed' from the congregation. The sinner never knew who struck the blow.

Wakeford believed that similar methods were used by the Dean against Miss Todhunter, the Principal of the Diocesan Training College for Schoolmistresses. Members of Miss Todhunter's staff were invited to protracted private interviews at the Deanery and, according to Wakeford, were encouraged to denigrate their Principal — so that Dr Fry could get rid of her.

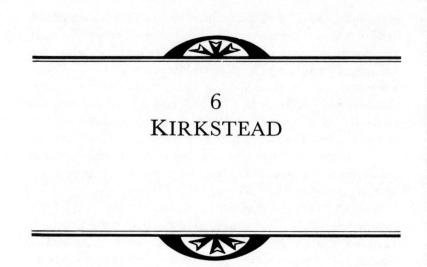

6
KIRKSTEAD

After two years of success in revitalising worship in the Cathedral at Lincoln, Wakeford found himself at a standstill, with Dean Fry firmly in control. Wakeford's oratory was still as compelling as ever, but jealous gossips were questioning his scholarship. Francis Woolley, the kindly assistant organist, knew what was going on. He recalled in his memoirs how Wakeford's frequent quotations from the early 'Fathers of the Church' were regarded with scepticism by Dr Fry and his cronies. They were largely incorrect, it was said, and mostly made up on the spur of the moment. For all his love of ceremony and symbolism, Wakeford was lampooned as a clumsy amateur. The improbable story went round the Close that he met the Bishop on Easter morning, who said, using the ancient salutation, 'Christ is Risen,' and Wakeford replied, 'Yes, Sir,' instead of producing the proper formula, 'He is Risen Indeed.'

Wakeford was never really accepted in the Close at Lincoln, even in the halcyon early months. He was not deliberately cold-shouldered, it was simply that he did not fit — either by background or temperament — into the closed little community that lived in the shadow of the Cathedral and which, in reality, was a kind of hot house where every move was observed, every social gaffe magnified by tittle-tattle and gossip.

It was noted that Archdeacon Wakeford was often away from home, and that when he was there they rarely entertained — except on the most formal occasions — and that Mrs Wakeford never stopped for a gossip in the Minster Yard, but just scuttled by on her way to the shops. And there was talk about the secretary, Evelyn Porter, the daughter of a brigadier, whom Wakeford had brought with him from Liverpool.

Isolated socially and brought to a halt in the Cathedral, Wakeford turned increasingly to his archdeaconry. It was large, containing twenty-one deaneries, stretching from the Humber southwards across the Lincolnshire Wolds and from the western lowlands at the Isle of Axholme to lonely sea marshes and Grimsby docks. George Jeudwine had worked hard in the archdeaconry, and had commissioned a survey of all the parsonage houses and glebe buildings in his charge. Wakeford was bent on further improvement. He bought a motor car, the better to keep his eye on things. Surprisingly, Dean Fry proposed that Wakeford should employ the son of his own chauffeur, Aurelius Popham (who had Dr Fry to thank for choosing his Christian name) — a friendly youth of about eighteen — to drive him and Wakeford agreed. It was not until some months later that Popham told Wakeford that Dr Fry had been interrogating him. According to Wakeford's later account, Popham had on many occasions been closely questioned about where he had been driving, what persons had been in the car and to whom the Archdeacon had spoken on the road.

Wakeford was horrified by what he saw as they chugged round the sprawling archdeaconry in the open-topped Rover during the last months before the First World War: neglected churches, dilapidated parsonages, weed-choked graveyards.

One incumbent of an isolated parish in the Wolds was running a harness business and the vicarage drive and churchyard walls were littered with the impedimenta of his trade.

Wakeford's most outrageous discovery was among the remains of a Cistercian Abbey near Woodhall Spa, some fifteen miles to the southeast of Lincoln. Woodhall Spa was an anomaly; a Bournemouth suburb dumped in dull Lincolnshire countryside, with two mock-Tudor hotels. Kirkstead Abbey was hardly less curious: a single pinnacle of crumbling masonry pointing like an accusing finger and, some distance away across a bumpy field, a solitary barn-like structure, oblong and semi-derelict, with an ancient steep-pitched roof. This last surviving building, the chapel *ante portas* of the Abbey, was now Kirkstead parish church, and it was in a shocking state. Yet despite its derelict condition and overgrown graveyard, it was an architectural treasure. Only forty feet by twenty, vaulted in beautiful, biscuit-coloured stone, it contained the marble effigy of a thirteenth-century knight in surcoat and visored helmet, and a notable circular Norman font. But in 1913 the interior was filthy and cobwebbed; the lancet windows were boarded up and the masonry cracking.

Surprisingly, in view of the state of the church, the Kirkstead Estate was owned by a clergyman. The Reverend Charles Thomas Moore was a parson of the old breed who had inherited the place from an aunt and used it mainly for sporting purposes. A staunch Tory who refused to read the prayer for Parliament when the Liberals were in office, Moore was Rector of Appleby Magna, a small village sixty miles away from Kirkstead, in the neighbouring diocese of Peterborough. Moore was as different from Wakeford as it is possible to imagine. Educated at Eton and Cambridge, he had been Rector of his Leicestershire parish since 1877. There had been Moores in or around Appleby since the sixteenth century, and the living was in the gift of the squire,

now Charles's elder brother George who lived comfortably at
Appleby Hall.

'Squire' Moore, as the Rector of Appleby Magna was
known in Kirkstead and Woodhall Spa, was sixty-seven years
of age in 1914 — a small, vigorous man with piercing eyes
and long side-whiskers who held himself stiffly erect and
whose passion in life was sport. As a young man he had been
fond of cock-fighting and point-to-point racing, and still
hunted regularly with the Atherstone over the gently
undulating country that skirted the Leicestershire coalfields.
He rarely wore clerical dress and was in every respect a
country gentleman — and a pretty racy one at that. Moore
had been known to arrive at his church hot from the chase,
leaving his horse outside, and take the service in hunting
pink.

In liturgical matters Moore differed entirely from Wakeford: Holy Communion was celebrated at Appleby Magna
only on the first Sunday of each month. Communion wafers
were not used. Moore preferred to carve up a loaf on the
dining-room table to make rough cubes of bread for the Host.
He was asked to cut the bread a little smaller when an elderly
female communicant nearly choked to death. After the
service, the Communion Plate was packed up in a wooden
box — there were no ritual ablutions — and carried back to
the Rectory for safe keeping in the Rector's bedroom.

Moore was greatly irritated if a funeral, wedding service or
christening at Appleby Magna interfered with Ascot, the
Grand National or the Eton and Harrow cricket match. He
was an enthusiastic Freemason of high degree and a member
of several local Lodges. Yet between his sporting activities
and freemasonry Moore served his people in a rough and
ready way. They understood their lusty parson and hugely enjoyed him singing the drinking song 'The Tars of Tarporley'
at the choir supper.

By an odd coincidence, Moore was the neighbour of
Herbert Worthington, Wakeford's fox-hunting brother-in-law.

Worthington had moved to the district from Cadeby in 1897, to become Rector of Seal, Netherseal and Overseal, and was now Rural Dean. His tall, redbrick rectory at Northseal was only five miles across the fields from Appleby Magna. Like Charles Moore, Worthington held a family living (his uncle William Worthington was Patron of Northseal and Lord of the Manor of Pype-cum-Membris). Despite extensive glebe land and a generous stipend of £993, he was up to his eyes in debt, for the Worthingtons were an extravagant couple and lived the life of country gentry, which meant they had to pay for a Curate as well as keeping hunters in the stables and a four-cylinder Belsize in the garage.

The Rector's financial scrapes were a recurring topic of interest in the village. The butcher had dunned Worthington for seventy pounds and received a cheque for ten. The organist was told, 'I can't pay you now — got to do a spot of fishing.' On the other hand, Worthington's generosity to the poor was renowned in Netherseal — 'Go and see old Worthington — he'll give you something.' He was a convivial man, preached a good sermon and enjoyed a pipe and bottle of the family ale in The Holly Bush. But he liked to have his own way, and was very put out if he failed to get it. It was said that Mrs Worthington was 'downtrodden' and bore all the worry of the Rector's daughter, Dorothy; the little girl had been born at the same time as her cousin John Wakeford and she was 'simple' and walked with a limp.

★ ★ ★

Worthington and Moore were the best of friends. They met regularly — on the hunting field and at the dining table. The tall figure of the Rector of Netherseal was a familiar sight in Appleby Magna as he rode over on church business or for a gossip with Mrs Moore. She learnt a good deal about Archdeacon Wakeford's private life. Worthington's dislike of his brother-in-law had grown by this time into loathing — and he didn't mind talking about it. They had met on only half-a-dozen occasions since Evelyn's wedding in Northlew twenty years before. The trouble was not only that the two men differed in almost every conceivable way, but, as Mrs Moore discovered, Worthington believed Wakeford had treated his sister badly. He became obsessed with the idea, largely as a result of some letters which Evelyn had written, at a time when she was apparently depressed, and he had convinced himself that Wakeford had risen to power at Lincoln at the cost of Evelyn's happiness. The scandal of the postman's wife, which George Wise had so carefully fomented, had also reached Worthington's ears and he was prepared to believe the worst of his brother-in-law, who was now lording it over the Lincolnshire countryside. Even the patrons of The Holly Bush were regaled with bitter details about the Archdeacon's supposed character.

Charles Moore was a singularly difficult man for Wakeford to oppose on the matter of Kirkstead church, for the Rector of Appleby Magna had a strong dislike of clerical authority, especially when it came from a cathedral close. During the early years of his rectorship his sporting activities had been reported to the Bishop of Peterborough, who had taken particular exception to Moore riding in point-to-point races, and told him so. This censure only increased Moore's hostility to bishops. The Archdeacon of Stow's visits were therefore not well received at Kirkstead. Wakeford complained vigorously about Moore's behaviour, referring to him as 'a dissolute parson of Leicestershire', who allowed the church of which he was patron to fall into ruin.

Moore was mystified and outraged by Wakeford's interference in his affairs. After all, the estate at Kirkstead was well run and the shooting was excellent. The 'old church' could only be reached by a muddy cart track; there was no living to go with it, no vicarage and no vicar, but he was quite willing to allow it to be opened for a local burial service or to admit an occasional visitor. That the Archdeacon

79

should make such a fuss was beyond his comprehension.

The Archdeacon, however, was determined to have his way and the Bishop of Lincoln supported him in his complaints. The upshot was a notable victory for Wakeford. On the 15th May 1915, a note appeared in *The Times* referring to some correspondence which had been published the previous year about the church at Kirkstead:

> 'Archdeacon Wakeford now writes — ''The church has remained closed for forty years past and has fallen gradually into a decay which promised final collapse. The care of this parish has now been laid upon me, and the preservation of the church has begun. Mr Weir, the well-known architect, has undertaken this work and has brought to it his trusted reverence and experience.'' '

The restoration was a fine achievement for Wakeford but it was less than wise of him to take on the Bishop's offer of the living of Kirkstead, with an income of £20 per annum to add to his stipends as Precentor of Lincoln Cathedral and Archdeacon of Stow. It was bound to embroil him further with the Rector of Appleby Magna and, in fact, he had to run the gauntlet of crossing Moore's property every time he wished to reach Kirkstead church.

The re-opening of the church was only the beginning of 'Squire' Moore's troubles. In the summer of 1915 he learned that he was to be ordered before a Consistory Court of the Diocese of Peterborough to answer 'certain charges of immoral conduct'.

Charles Moore was devastated by this second blow. His son recalled that for a couple of days his father 'simply did not know what to do'. In desperation, Moore drove across from Appleby to the nearby coalfield village of Heather to seek the help of a brother Mason. Harry Ford was a breezy bachelor, a prominent figure on the hunting field astride his great grey horse, the Baron; he was also the owner of a prosperous brick yard and Moore respected his practical shrewdness. Ford

calmed the shaken rector and then took him to a lawyer in
West Bromwich. Back in Appleby Magna, the support of his
capable wife and the staunch friendship of his neighbour
Worthington helped Moore to face the ordeal.

★　　★　　★

The trial was held in the Old Town Hall at Leicester, before
the Chancellor of the Diocese of Peterborough, Sir Alfred
Kemp, and five assessors. It was alleged that 'on 17th March
last and on other occasions within the last five years Moore
was guilty of immoral conduct with a woman named Mary
Ratcliffe at a house in Lincoln.' According to the prosecuting
counsel, 'the woman Ratcliffe' had been married in 1879,
and had then left her husband and gone to live with a man
named Ellis who was employed 'as a sort of caretaker' at
Kirkstead House. Counsel was unable to say whether the
acquaintance between Moore and the woman had begun after
he had taken on Ellis or whether the employment of the man
was consequent upon Moore's immoral association with the
woman. At that time, 'Daisy' Ratcliffe was well on in middle
years and extremely fat. The court learned that she was
frequently to be seen driving off to the races with Moore.
They had also been observed in a room at Kirkstead House
'with glasses before them', though 'there was no allegation
that misconduct had actually taken place there'.

Moore's counsel said that the train service between
Appleby Magna and Kirkstead was notoriously bad; his client
had been in the habit of leaving Appleby at mid-day,
spending the night in Lincoln and then going on to Kirkstead
the following morning. For about four years Moore had put
up at 21 Vine Street, Lincoln, in lodgings run by 'Daisy'
Ratcliffe. He had told his wife what he was doing and had not
the slightest suspicion that the house was not a proper place to
stay. The defendant was 'an old fashioned clergyman and had
always been among horses'. He had never in his life been to

Lincoln races with 'Mrs Ellis'. He argued that Moore was not guilty in the remotest degree of any of the charges. Mr Moore was sixty-eight years of age, said counsel — a fact in itself, he would have thought, almost enough to make charges of this kind impossible.

The court adjourned after Moore had given his evidence. The following morning there was an unexpected development. Counsel for the prosecution stood up to announce that although 21 Vine Street was without question a house of ill-repute, and the defendant had admitted visiting it frequently, he had been instructed by the Bishop of Peterborough to accept the evidence given by the defendant. Moore's counsel claimed that it was 'an acquittal in the extremest form', although it must have strained the credulity of the court that Moore — a worldly man if ever there was one — could have been a regular guest in a bawdy house without recognising it as such. But the Rector of Appleby Magna was cleared of the charge of immorality with 'Daisy' Ratcliffe.

The Consistory Court case had been a dreadful experience for the Moores. On the last day of the hearing Mrs Moore collapsed on the platform of Leicester station with a stroke. She was never entirely well again.

Moore laid the responsibility for his wife's condition — and his other recent troubles — on the Archdeacon of Stow who, he was convinced, was behind the charges against him. He was outraged by what he saw as Wakeford's hypocrisy. Moore firmly believed that John Wakeford was a jumped-up high-church womaniser, an arrogant and insufferable man who had brought nothing but unhappiness to his friend Worthington's sister. Furthermore, as Patron of Kirkstead, Moore was incensed at having to pay Wakeford's twenty pound stipend as vicar as well as having to endure him traipsing across his meadows to get to the church. It was therefore some satisfaction to him to make Wakeford's visits as unpleasant as possible — indeed, to try and scare him off.

There was an occasion when Wakeford and his wife were

crossing a path to the church: 'C.T. Moore appeared with two labouring men, who put themselves in front of us, and physically hindered us from going to the church. When we turned to go round they turned to come in front of us. Of course we would not fight, and eventually had to return by the road. I said to him: "If there is no right of way, why not take it to the courts?" He said, "Oh well; I'll have you after all, however long I wait." '

It is not clear if Wakeford knew what lay behind this threat; but from that time Moore was determined to destroy him. In Lincoln, Wakeford's enemy Dean Fry had much the same intention, but in this case Wakeford believed he knew what was going on.

★   ★   ★

In the spring of 1915, Wakeford developed psoriasis and his doctor sent him to a nursing home in Harrogate for treatment. Wakeford was there from the 17th to the 21st May of that year. Dean Fry used his absence as an opportunity for a campaign to prevent Wakeford's appointment as Visitor of a War Hospital in Lincoln. Fry's interference was thorough and Wakeford in the end declined to accept the post.

During Fry's whispering campaign 'a suggestion was made about Lincoln that I was not alone in Harrogate,' Wakeford wrote years later. 'On 6th July the Bishop referred to the Hospital, and said that there was some talk in connection with that which affirmed that when I was in Harrogate I had a companion with me from Lincoln.' Bishop Hicks, in his kindly way, assured Wakeford that it was all 'trivial and indefinite', but said that he had been visited by an old lady, who was 'difficult to understand', sent by Dean Fry to tell the Bishop about the supposed affair at Harrogate. Wakeford protested that the register of the nursing home at Harrogate was available for all to see and showed 'what persons were in that house during my stay'. He believed that he had convinced the Bishop of his innocence, but there were many in the diocese of Lincoln who were not convinced. The story of the Archdeacon's supposed exploits in Harrogate went round the rural deaneries of Lincolnshire. According to Wakeford it was flung at him as a jibe by the 'dissolute parson of Leicestershire' when he was trying to cross Moore's fields to Kirkstead church. And there was still talk of Evelyn Porter, the intense and devout young lady Wakeford had brought with him as his secretary from Liverpool.

Wakeford was by now as controversial a figure in Lincolnshire as he had been in Devon, and in the worst days at Liverpool. Clearly, there were many who liked and respected him. As the reporter of the *Liverpool Review* had sensed more than twenty years before, he combined a volcanic energy with occasional flashes of such singular sweetness as 'took the heart by storm'. He still had the support of his Bishop, despite all the gossip and sneering in the Close; the cathedral staff liked him and tolerated his autocratic ways and he was still on the best of terms with Dr Bennett. However Wakeford's enemies were growing in number and his occasional rash acts, such as preaching vigorously against the sin of simony at the induction of the Rector of Claxby-cum-Normanby-le-Wold, led to further unpopularity in the archdeaconry. So did his high-handed treatment of the Vicar of Wispington.

The Reverend James Penny was a timid one-eyed bachelor, who had been forced by Wakeford to celebrate a full complement of services even though his church was almost always empty. When a cataract badly affected the sight of his other eye, Penny resigned the living and retired to Woodhall Spa where, to his great distress, Wakeford continued to pursue him, to pay for the renovation costs of the vicarage at Wispington which Penny had allowed to fall into disrepair. Penny feared how this would be achieved: 'I have no doubt if he cannot do it legally the Archdeacon will try to bully me into doing it on moral, spiritual and religious grounds.'

However, Wakeford — impulsive as ever — got more than he bargained for in Woodhall Spa, as Mr Penny gleefully recounted:

'The Archdeacon made a disgraceful exhibition of himself here a week ago, as on seeing him, a small boy said to another, "There is another Mason out of work." Where upon the Archdeacon rushed at the boy, dragged him into the biggest shop, Chapmans, where the four crossroads meet near the Vicarage, and before a shop full of people raved and stormed at the boy — who feeling the eyes of Woodhall were on him, could only answer, "You looked like it and I thought you was out of work." Then the Archdeacon and he departs their several ways. And Woodhall is proud of its young hero.'

There was no middle way with John Wakeford: you were either for him or against him. To poor Mr Penny, he was an unfeeling bully; to C.T. Moore, a pious, meddling hypocrite; to Dean Fry, he was a dangerous radical, the Bishop's pawn, and a challenge to Fry's own authority in the Cathedral.

Although he could inspire such extreme responses — of love and admiration as well as hatred — Wakeford was not a chameleon. He was a firm and decisive man, whose impetuosity could nevertheless lead to absurd public altercations as well as winning the hearts of those who knew him best. The antagonisms that he evoked were not so much against Wakeford the man as against what he stood for. His reputation as an ogre was really compounded from a whiff of Roman incense and the clinging lies manufactured by George Wise about the high-church womaniser. There was also a disturbing streak of radicalism in him and he had the uncomfortable image of an over-zealous martinet troubling some lackadaisical parsons in his archdeaconry.

★   ★   ★

Bishop Hicks, in common with many Christian pacifists, believed that the First World War was 'the sport of a corrupt band of financiers, armament makers and imperial filibusters, made popular through an equally corrupt Press'. His care was for the injured; he moved with his family to a humble priest-vicar's house, just outside the Minster Gate, and the Palace became a Red Cross Hospital. The Bishop's three sons were in the Army: one was killed in France, another fought in Mesopotamia, a third was invalided out of Gallipoli and then wounded in France. Chancellor Johnston's son died on active service; Wakeford's son, John, left for the Royal Engineers in 1917. Every issue of the *Berkhamstedian* magazine brought news to the Deanery of the deaths of scores of Dean Fry's former pupils on the Western Front. Archdeacon Wakeford preached to the crews of the North Sea minesweepers at Grimsby Docks.

The routine of the Cathedral continued and there were those who said that the quarrels and rumours surrounding the Archdeacon of Stow hastened the Bishop's final illness. Wakeford had become a millstone around the Bishop's neck. In the spring following the end of the war, Hicks was weak and mortally ill. Not only was he tormented with hints from Dean Fry of Wakeford's association with a Lincoln woman, but he felt impelled to intervene on behalf of a clergyman whom Wakeford had accused of breaking the law by inviting a woman to preach at Evensong in his church.

In July 1919 Bishop Hicks resigned. His heart could not stand the strain. He died the following month in Worthing.

★ ★ ★

According to the Cathedral Statutes, a meeting of the Dean and Canons had to be convened to elect a Custodian of the Diocese, who would hold office until the new Bishop was enthroned. It was necessary to elect two candidates, one of whom would be chosen for this office by the Archbishop. In spite of the gossip, John Wakeford was unanimously elected, together with Dean Fry. The Archbishop chose Fry.

William Shuckburgh Swayne, the fifty-eight-year-old Dean of Manchester, was installed as Bishop of Lincoln in January 1920. Swayne had been an army chaplain in the South African War and on the Western Front. In his prime he had been something of a pugilist. Although his hair was greying, Swayne was a vigorous man, with a large nose, bushy eyebrows and a deep sonorous voice. In his early months at Lincoln, he relied heavily on the experience and advice of two subordinates: Canon Boulter (whom Swayne inherited as Bishop's Secretary) and Dean Fry. Boulter knew the Diocese intimately and Swayne was soon deeply involved in its affairs; Fry with his experience and hard-won authority in the Chapter became a valued confidant. John Wakeford could make little headway with Swayne and soon realised the extent of the Dean's influence over the new Bishop: 'he was infected and stupefied before he was three months in the Diocese,' Wakeford wrote later.

Wakeford reacted by bringing into his sermons and lectures an intensity and ardour even beyond that which he customarily showed. In less than a month, and in addition to all his archidiaconal responsibilities, he delivered forty-five sermons and addresses, fourteen of them in six days, and there was the prospect of six lectures on pastoral theology at Durham University as well as five sermons to be given to congregations of businessmen at Liverpool in the last week of March.

As he wrote his Durham lectures, Wakeford's mind was on the problem of clerical discipline. He did not consider the matter from the point of view of an erring priest; he was concerned with the prosecution of justice. He would have been stunned to know how soon his words would describe his own case:

'How often do we hear now of one or other of the clergy who acts by himself and for himself without regard to the consequences that his neighbours may suffer from his irregularity or impulsiveness. Sometimes it seems to be a thirst for popularity, and sometimes a strange desire to provoke hostility, and sometimes an ambition to have the applause of the newspapers, and sometimes — most prolific cause of all — simple stupidity: but whatever the cause may be, the difficulty exists up and down the country, one man reckless or misguided, imposing the penalty of his unrestraint upon ten or fifteen others, wiser or kindlier than himself. If any one of us contemplates an adventure which is going to reflect upon or embarrass his brethren, his plain duty is to bring the matter first into Chapter and ask for conference.'

John Wakeford portrayed in *Some Liverpool Celebrities*

PART THREE

WAKEFORD
contra mundum

7
LEAVE TO APPEAL

The news that the Archdeacon of Stow was to be tried for immorality had all Lincoln by the ears. There had never been anything like this in the history of the Cathedral.

In the days before the Consistory Court hearing people greeted the Archdeacon as a pariah, avoiding him in the steep streets or passing him with averted eyes in the Close. Hostility was not confined to the cathedral set: the citizens took sides and pro- and anti-Wakeford factions developed among tradesmen, working men and professional people alike. A visitor to Lincoln at the time described the antagonism:

> 'Strolling into the town, I heard, as two large and, by their appearances, affluent individuals passed by with loud remarks on the case, ''Got him? I should think they have got him. I hope they'll ... '' I followed these worthies, and the conversation was a fugue. ''He'd ordered a private room. They got him. I hope they'll ... '' These remarks were addressed in the loudest tones, not without oaths, to the street.'

Wakeford even had enemies among those who were to pass

judgment on him, not only Dean Fry, who had charge of the arrangements for the trial, but also among the assessors of the Consistory Court itself. There was the Vicar of Grimsby, who Wakeford believed had spread scandal about him in the archdeaconry, and Canon Akenhead, Vicar of St Martin's in Lincoln. On the evening before the trial, Akenhead, a thin gloomy man with a drooping walrus moustache, had stopped to gossip with a city alderman.

They talked about Wakeford. It was a cold February evening. 'I cannot believe him to be guilty,' the alderman said.

'I know one thing,' Wakeford's assessor replied, 'I shall not believe a word he says.'

There were others who were steadfast friends, none more so than Edward Leeke. The Sub-Dean did not take sides. He 'expressed no opinion, in public, as to "guilty" or "not guilty",' an acquaintance recalled: 'he befriended a soul that he realised must be suffering great anguish.' Leeke's friendship and charity did not waver throughout Wakeford's long ordeal, for that good man was privately convinced of Wakeford's innocence.

★　　★　　★

The verdict of the Consistory Court caused wild excitement. The newspapers had a field day, not only with headlines announcing the outcome — 'ARCHDEACON GUILTY'; 'DRAMATIC VERDICT OF A CONSISTORY COURT' — but with accounts of Wakeford's defiance: 'ARCHDEACON UNDAUNTED', 'I AM NOT ASKING FOR PITY, I ONLY WANT JUSTICE'; 'WIFE'S STAUNCH FAITH IN HER HUSBAND'S INNOCENCE'.

Letters of support poured into the Precentory from all over the country. Thirty of Wakeford's parishioners at Kirkstead wrote to tell him they thought him falsely accused; two businessmen travelled from London to offer their help; a fund was started in Liverpool to launch an appeal, and within five days had reached £1,800. Others were opened in London and Suffolk. The servants at the Precentory offered to sacrifice their wages and the Cathedral choir boys sent two pounds ten shillings.

Sub-Dean Leeke and a Lincoln vicar, the Rector of Horncastle, wrote a letter to the *Lincoln Chronicle* announcing that a subscription list had been opened to help Archdeacon Wakeford cover the costs of an appeal. A letter from a Reading doctor appeared in the same newspaper, recording his dismay at the verdict: 'I will not allude to the motives and proceedings of the Archdeacon's accusers. Of these a discriminating public can judge as well as I. They will, I think, agree with me that in accordance with our experience of human conduct, a grave injustice has been perpetrated.'

Evelyn Wakeford gave a press interview. 'One of the most painful things about the case to me,' she was reported as saying, 'is the suggestion that there are differences between myself and my husband. I am appalled to hear that there are doubts as to whether I am personally convinced of his innocence. I was never so convinced of anything in the world as that such a thing as has been charged against him is utterly impossible.'

'I am not a fool,' she continued, 'and I am not a woman who would defend a man at any price — even to save the honour of my house — but I have known my husband for thirty-four years, and during that time he has had only two ideas, his devotion to the Church and his devotion to his wife. I appeal to those who know me, and who believe with me, to help, if they can, in clearing the name of the man I love.'

Wakeford was close to despair. 'People are inclined to drop their hands and make lamentations,' he said, 'but it is nothing to the world whether one man goes up or down.' Most galling was his exclusion from the Cathedral and from his archdeaconry: he could not bear to be absent from his work of preaching the gospel 'even for a day'.

One of Wakeford's sympathisers was a friend of the alderman who had chatted with Canon Akenhead on the evening before the trial. Councillor Baker was a boisterous, hail-fellow-well-met sort of man and, when he next met Akenhead, he asked bluntly: had he told Alderman Footman that he would not believe a word that Wakeford would say?

'I might have done,' came the reply.

'Did you say it,' Baker persisted. 'Yes or no?'

'Yes I did,' said the Canon.

Baker realised that he had clear evidence that an assessor had pre-judged the case and hurried off to tell Wakeford about it.

The most unexpected offer of help came from the haggard young man who had waited with his pale bedraggled wife in the crowded hotel lobby on the evening of the Peterborough Horse Fair. The poet, Edmund Blunden, had followed the newspaper accounts of the Wakeford trial with astonishment and realised that he himself had been an actor in the drama. Blunden had walked into the Bull Hotel with his wife, Mary, on the evening of the 15th March. They were soaked to the skin. With his friend Alan Porter, Blunden had discovered the remarkable collection of manuscripts by the poet John Clare hidden away in the Peterborough Natural History Museum, and the young writer and his pregnant wife had come to work on them. All the hotels were full and he and Mary tramped around for most of the afternoon in a fruitless search for lodgings. They came finally to the Bull and waited dejectedly — first in the bar and then by the staircase — until the manager's harassed wife at last told them that they could have a room. They dined in the hotel that night and noticed the Archdeacon when Mary Blunden was drying her furs at the grill room fire at breakfast time the following day.

The Blundens told Wakeford's solicitor everything they knew, and so did a number of other guests, including the horse dealers and farmers who had noticed the 'old parson' in the dining-room at the time of the Horse Fair.

Wakeford's counsel prepared the case for an appeal. Application was made to the Judicial Committee of the Privy Council. This was arguably the most remarkable court the world has ever known; at that time it held sway over the lives, liberties and properties of more than a quarter of the inhabitants of the planet. It was empowered to hear every kind of cause — civil, criminal, international or constitutional — and to apply almost every conceivable kind of law, from the Napoleonic Code of Mauritius to Chinese Law from the British Courts in Canton. The Judicial Committee was also required to arbitrate in appeals from English Ecclesiastical Courts.

Wakeford's appeal was heard on Monday, 28th February 1921, in the tall, oak-panelled chamber of the Privy Council at 9 Downing Street. Four lords of appeal sat in lounge suits without their robes behind a long, polished table at the centre of the crowded room. In the middle was the Lord Chancellor, Birkenhead. On his right were the lords Buckmaster and Shaw; and on his left was Lord Dunedin. Ranged behind them were the ecclesiastical assessors: the bishops of London, Gloucester, Rochester and Ely, in gaiters and frock-coats, seated on oak chairs in a row against the wall. Jammed in the press of spectators at the back of the crowded room, his top hat on his knee, was the Rector of Appleby, Charles Moore.

Wakeford's counsel, Sir Marlay Samson K.C., standing wigged and gowned in the small wooden-railed enclosure immediately in front of the law lords, told the Committee that there were three grounds which supported the application to appeal. First, the judgment was not in accordance with the true facts; secondly, fresh evidence had been discovered since the trial; thirdly, one of the assessors of the Consistory Court had been guilty of misconduct, in that he had pre-judged the issue.

Sir Marlay dealt with the third ground first. He placed on the table two affidavits: one sworn by Alderman Footman, the other by Councillor Baker. These affirmed Canon

Akenhead's prior refusal to believe the defendant's evidence in the Consistory Court. This, Sir Marlay submitted, was 'misconduct that would vitiate the trial,' for an assessor was 'in a position of a member of a jury' and 'must bring an unbiased mind to bear.' Furthermore, Sir Marlay argued, 'the evidence of the witnesses for the prosecution shows such grave discrepancies, and is so negatived by the evidence of those for the defence, as prima facie to make out a case for further investigation.'

Counsel elaborated on the dubious part played by a detective, Agar, and by his employer, Charles Moore.

'Do I understand you to say that the whole of the evidence from beginning to end is a tissue of falsehood?' Lord Buckmaster enquired.

'I am put in that position by my client,' Samson replied.

The elusive girl in the Cathedral had been sought, but as Samson was forced to admit he would not be in a position 'to inform the Court that we shall be able to call this fresh evidence'.

'It comes to this, you abandon one of your claims,' the Lord Chancellor interjected.

Counsel demurred, for there was a Mr Blunden who would be called to give evidence 'which was now material'. The law lords and the four bishops were convinced. The Lord Chancellor announced their decision.

'Their lordships have formed the view that there are respects in which the matter might have been more fully investigated, having regard to its gravity. There are also circumstances in the case which have caused their lordships some anxiety. Their decision is to re-hear this matter by way of an appeal.'

Wakeford had won the chance to fight again.

8

THE HEARING

It seemed a good omen that Lord Birkenhead would preside
at the hearing. The Lord Chancellor had been born and bred
in Liverpool and had represented the city in Parliament. He
was a self-made man (so he liked to portray himself) and
Wakeford felt an unbounded admiration for him: despite the
fact that, as F.E. Smith, the up-and-coming M.P. and
Liverpool barrister, he had vigorously espoused the
Protestant cause and been the defender of George Wise.
Birkenhead was a dissipated, sardonic politician described as
'without question the most fascinating creature of his time'.
In 1921 he was at the height of his power. He was forty-eight
at the time of the Wakeford Case and lived only another nine
years, but in his relatively brief career 'F.E.' had probably
encompassed more than any of his eminent contemporaries in
the early decades of the century. As a lawyer, he was a
brilliant advocate and an outstanding Lord Chancellor; as a
politician, a devastating debater and a wily tactician; to his
friends, who ranged from Horatio Bottomley to Winston
Churchill, he was loyal, exuberant and generous. But his
genius was flawed by crude ruthlessness and extravagance. It

was said of him: 'many people loved him, most distrusted him, some despised him, and he despised almost everyone. In his later career as Lord Birkenhead he served himself more faithfully than his God or his country'.

Another participant in the trial was hardly less brilliant. The former Solicitor-General, Sir Edward Carson, had been instructed to lead Sir Marlay Samson K.C. for Wakeford's defence. Carson, a tall, lantern-jawed hypochondriac Ulsterman, had had a meteoric and turbulent career. In 1895 he was counsel for the prosecution in the trial of Oscar Wilde. In 1911 he came close to treason in his support for the Orange cause in Ireland. Birkenhead (then nicknamed 'Orange' or 'Galloper' Smith) had been Carson's leading lieutenant and had roared threats of armed rebellion from many public platforms in Ulster. In 1912, the two men had sailed back to Liverpool together to a dockside reception from 150,000 cheering supporters.

The Wakeford Case was the last which Carson would ever lead, for within a month he was to take his seat as a Lord of Appeal in that court.

By an odd chance, Wakeford's was also the last case in which Douglas Hogg would appear before becoming Attorney-General. Hogg (later Viscount Hailsham, Lord Chancellor) had been briefed to represent the Bishop of Lincoln, together with the Chancellor of the Diocese (later Sir William Hansell) and William Stable (later Mr Justice Stable) as Hogg's junior. A straightforward and uncomplicated man of cheerful disposition, Douglas Hogg was a supreme advocate and never more so than at Wakeford's appeal.

★   ★   ★

On the morning of the 7th April 1921, for the first time in the history of the Judicial Committee of the Privy Council, a long queue formed in Downing Street, with clergymen and fur-coated women jostling witnesses and newspapermen for entry to the court. So great was the crush in the chamber that the Archdeacon and his wife were forced to squash in with the spectators at the back of the chamber. Crowded together behind the four law lords, seated at a long mahogany table with square, Queen Anne silver inkwells, was a group of especially privileged onlookers.

The proceedings were opened by Douglas Hogg, a comfortable tubby figure who explained that it was not disputed that Archdeacon Wakeford had stayed at the Bull Hotel, Peterborough, on two occasions. The question was whether he was accompanied by a woman.

In clear, measured tones Hogg recounted to the packed assembly the prosecution's version of Wakeford's supposed adventures in Peterborough: how the Archdeacon had been seen with a woman in the Cathedral and later, as new evidence would show, had visited a tapestry school in Peterborough, still in the company of a woman; how the hotel books were kept; how Mr Pugh received a postcard booking a double room for Good Friday; how Wakeford had reappeared, again with a woman; how the hotel register had been carried up to the bedroom by Mrs Pugh, to be signed by the woman and how Wakeford had said it was not necessary, but had the next morning written in 'The Precincts, Lincoln' and then inserted the words 'and wife'.

Charles Pugh, the hotel manager, was the first witness to appear at the wooden lectern in front of Birkenhead. He told Douglas Hogg that he had entered the name 'Eartford' against Room 15 in the tabular book (for meals taken), having copied it from the hotel register, and that he had received a telephone enquiry from the police station about the identity of the clerical visitor. Not being able to decipher the name in the visitors' book, he had gone up to the bedroom and found the name 'Wakeford' on the pyjamas. Pugh explained that he had asked the Archdeacon on the Monday evening to add the words 'The Precincts, Lincoln' to the hotel register. The witness then went on to confirm the details of the Archdeacon's second visit to the hotel with the woman, signing: 'J. Wakeford and wife, Precincts, Lincoln' with, immediately below, 'M. Wakeford'.

The hotel books were produced by Mr Pugh and passed across to the law lords and then to the bishops, each of whom peered in turn through a magnifying glass at the signatures in the register; then they examined the Archdeacon's hotel bill for the March visit, which amounted to £4.2s.6d.

Sir Edward Carson started his cross-examination innocently enough by asking Mr Pugh how long he had been at the Bull Hotel. He had only gone there in the February of the previous year from Glasgow, came the reply. Before that he had been in the Army. Why had he now left the Bull Hotel, Carson enquired?

'That is my business...' Pugh blurted out.

'You must not speak to learned counsel like that,' Birkenhead admonished him, 'you must answer his questions.'

Pugh then admitted that he had left as the result of a disagreement with the owner of the hotel. Carson knew this and was trying to shake the credibility of the witness. Pugh was later cross-examined about the visit of the police to the hotel. Carson pressed him hard, his powerful Irish voice filling the chamber.

'I put it to you that the police were looking for a clergyman with a lady who, it was alleged, had shortly before been giving bogus cheques.'

'That information I got subsequently. At the time I knew nothing,' Pugh answered.

'Who gave you the information?'

'Sergeant King. He told me that the clergyman was going about uttering false cheques.'

'Do you know that it was an incident that happened four years ago, and for which the particular clergyman was in gaol at the time?'

'I don't know.'

After luncheon, Pugh returned to his ordeal with Carson, who managed to extract a description of Wakeford's supposed companion from the reluctant witness. She was aged about thirty, and had been dressed in a blue costume, with a dark hat, and was about five feet six inches tall, Pugh said. Carson then pressed him on the matter of the entry in the visitors' book, 'J. Wakeford and wife'.

'I put it to you that you also wrote that "and wife",' Carson challenged.

'You are wrong, Sir; it was written before he left.'

'Why did you write it?' Carson persisted.

'Because I concluded that she was his wife, but I don't know why I wrote the words in.'

Carson had broken through. The spectators in the stuffy chamber hung on his words as he bludgeoned Pugh with a rapid sequence of questions, trying to show that the hotel register and accounts had been carelessly kept. Then he switched his questioning back to the woman. Wakeford was listening intently, shifting restlessly in his seat. Suddenly, the court was galvanised by Carson rounding on Pugh, a slight figure beside the tall, dishevelled lawyer, and saying sharply, 'Have you seen this woman since?'

'I have seen somebody resembling her,' Pugh replied.

'Where?'

'It was at Great Marlborough Street Police Station.'

'When?'

'About a fortnight ago.'

'Did you point her out to anyone?'

'No.'

Carson rattled out questions like a machine gun until Pugh had difficulty keeping up.

'Did not your wife go into her room at the police court — the room of the court missionary — and say "This is the Lady"?'

'I don't know, I was outside at the time.'

The crowded room was in a fever of excitement; such was

101

the impact of Carson's battering. Wakeford's face was flushed as he sat, quite motionless now, with his hands folded across his chest.

'Is it not alleged that this court missionary is the lady of the occasion?' Carson demanded.

Pugh hesitated, then blurted out, 'She resembled the lady. I am not prepared to swear on oath that she was the lady.'

Carson continued his demolition work on the evidence of Pugh's wife, a smartly dressed little woman with her face almost hidden by a large cloche hat. Carson returned repeatedly to the matter of the Archdeacon's pyjamas.

'Instead of peering into an old clergyman's night clothes, why did you not ask him his name?'

'I could not read it in the book,' replied Mrs Pugh in her strong Scottish accent.

'Have you ever gone up before to examine the night clothes of guests?'

'No.'

'Don't you think it was a peculiar thing to do?'

'No.'

Mrs Pugh's denial ended the proceedings. It had been a good day for Carson; the Pughs' evidence now looked threadbare.

★   ★   ★

The following morning, people queued again in Downing Street — this time in semi-darkness with evening bird-song and stars shining overhead: there was an eclipse of the sun. Among the crowds in the half-light were armed secret service men, in case of trouble from Sinn Fein.

Sir Edward Carson soon disposed of Mrs Pugh, but not before he had extracted from her the admission that she could not swear to the identity of the woman she had seen at Marlborough Street Police Station and, furthermore, that the woman had not recognised her.

Fanny Willcocks, the chambermaid, gave her evidence to Hogg under Sir Edward Carson's hostile stare. She said, 'the gentleman had night attire on the Sunday evening. The lady had none.' She maintained that in the bedroom she had heard the gentleman tell the woman to 'frankly deny' that she had stayed with him. In the dining-room she had heard the Archdeacon tell the woman, 'take your hands off the table or it will give the show away.'

'I then noticed she had no wedding ring,' Mrs Willcocks explained.

'Did you not think it strange that a clergyman, there for immoral purposes, should talk thus openly before you?' enquired Sir Edward.

'It never occurred to me,' Willcocks paused, 'he neither shouted nor whispered.'

Mr Frank Tuplin, the drapery manager from the Co-op was the next witness to appear, and gave his version of events to Douglas Hogg.

Cross-examined by Carson, Tuplin said that he knew Archdeacon Wakeford by sight, having once lived in Lincoln himself. He had been in the Bull on both occasions when Wakeford had arrived. According to Frank Tuplin, Pugh had said to him, 'Don't you know who that is? That is Archdeacon Wakeford.'

'Then on the Sunday evening, the manager must have known that it was Archdeacon Wakeford?' Carson enquired.

'Yes, I should think so,' Tuplin agreed. He admitted that he knew a Mrs Ellis who had lived in Lincoln sixteen years before.

'Did you know that Mrs Ellis is a lady who, it is suggested, kept an immoral house in Lincoln?'

'Yes.'

'Do you know that a clergyman of the name of Moore had a charge made against him of stopping in her house?'

'I was told that at Lincoln.'

After a slight brush with Douglas Hogg, concerning the

103

withdrawal of charges against Moore at the Consistory Court, Carson managed to get out of Tuplin that he knew Archdeacon Wakeford had supplied the information which had led to Moore's trial.

Police-Sergeant King, in his evidence, said that on the 15th March he saw the Archdeacon and a young woman together in Westgate and watched them go into the Bull Hotel. The Archdeacon went into the hotel office and signed the visitors' book, while the woman waited in the passage. About three weeks later he saw the same two persons again, walking towards the Bull Hotel. Passing them he reached the hotel first, and was there when they both signed the visitors' book.

When cross-examined by Sir Edward Carson, King admitted that the clergyman who had been passing false cheques had, in fact, been gaoled in 1917. He said that it was a mistake when the police had said that they were on the look out for such a person.

Police-Constable Hall and Detective-Sergeant Smith also testified that they saw the Archdeacon, with a woman, near the Bull Hotel on their second visit. P.C. Hall remembered being spoken to in the street by the Archdeacon on the 15th March, when he asked where he could obtain a hot bath. The Constable said that he directed the Archdeacon and his companion to the Grand Hotel, which he saw them enter.

The Dean of Peterborough then gave evidence of having seen Archdeacon Wakeford in the Cathedral with a lady at the time of the Diocesan Conference in March 1920. He recalled that Sergeant King had come to him later to enquire about the 'Bishop' who was staying at the Bull Hotel.

There was a stir of interest in the Court when Herbert Worthington was called, an elegant monocled figure, tall in a grey frock-coat. He related in a clear, languid voice his part in bringing his brother-in-law to trial, how he had heard rumours of Wakeford's visit to Peterborough, had inspected the register of the Bull Hotel and reported the matter to the Bishop of Peterborough.

Edward Carson cross-examined Worthington closely about his relationship with C.T. Moore and his part in bringing charges against his brother-in-law. Worthington said that he saw his sister about the case in July.

'Why did you wait until July 5th?' Carson demanded.

'I wanted to be sure of certain facts.'

'Why did you not write to your sister and say, "A serious matter has arisen about Wakeford, your husband, which will bring him down and you, and I want to know is there any explanation?" Did it not occur to you as a Christian man?'

'No, I thought I should see her sooner or later.'

'Did you say to your sister that John Wakeford and a woman slept at the Bull Hotel and signed the register on March 14th, 1920?'

'I did not say the date, I said he had slept there.'

'Did you tell her there were grave rumours against John Wakeford's morality?'

'I did,' said Worthington, 'I told her that I had seen his signature with "and wife" in the hotel book, and that was strong enough for me. I wanted no other witnesses.'

'Did you tell her,' asked Sir Edward, 'that Mr Moore said he intended some day to get John Wakeford and would do it easily if he waited patiently?'

'I did not,' replied Worthington.

The cross-examination turned to the identity of Wakeford's alleged companion.

'Whom did you suspect?' Carson asked.

'A lady named Evelyn Porter.'

There was a murmur of excitement in the court. Wakeford — his face lined and pallid — listened intently from a place behind the solicitor's table.

'Is that the lady who is the court missionary at Great Marlborough Street?' Sir Edward enquired.

'I have not the faintest notion who she is. I have never seen her.'

Later Carson switched his questioning back to Worthington's relationship with C.T. Moore. 'Was it Moore who gave you the statements of Pugh, Mrs Pugh and the chambermaid of the hotel?'

'It was.'

'Was it Moore who employed Detective Agar?'

'He sent him to help me.'

'That is what I call employing. Why should Moore employ detectives to hunt down people?'

'He was not a detective.'

'Well, he is an ex-policeman. Who paid him?'

'I have not paid him.'

According to Worthington, Moore did not pay Agar either. Only his expenses: two pounds eighteen shillings in all. Worthington reluctantly revealed that Agar had married Moore's cook 'many years ago'. As far as Worthington knew, his neighbour had never before made any charges against Wakeford.

'Had he made any to you about Miss Porter?' Carson asked.

'No.'

'Who made them?'

'My sister.'

Worthington maintained that Evelyn Wakeford had complained to him about Evelyn Porter on 'every occasion' that they had met during the previous fifteen years.

Finally, Sir Edward was anxious to learn about Worthington's relationship with his brother-in-law.

'I believe he has been married about twenty-eight years, and I have only seen him five or six times in my life. We were not particularly friends but we had no quarrels,' said Mr Worthington.

'Just ordinary Christian friendship between two clergymen?' Carson said in his harsh drawl.

'No, I would not put it as high as that,' Worthington replied laconically and there was laughter.

This was the end of the second day of the appeal. It had

been another success for Carson. He had been faced with a daunting array of evidence against his client, but with a combination of wit, blarney and audacity had dominated the Court and made Douglas Hogg's witnesses look extremely unreliable. Furthermore, as Hogg's junior, William Stable, felt, the sympathy of the Court was running strongly for Wakeford. Stable sensed this not only among the packed spectators but even with the Lord Chancellor himself.

★   ★   ★

But, on the following morning the tide seemed to turn as Douglas Hogg produced, one after another, a string of witnesses who swore to the presence of a woman with the Archdeacon in Peterborough.

A Miss Adelaide Weston, who ran a tapestry school close to the Cathedral in Peterborough, said that she had seen Archdeacon Wakeford with a woman in the workroom of her school in March 1920. She remembered the occasion 'because there was a snowstorm at the time', the woman was young, fairly tall and dressed in dark clothes.

Miss Adams, who worked at the tapestry school, said that she too remembered the day of the snowstorm in March 1920, when a clergyman came into the workroom with a young woman. They came soon after eleven o'clock and stayed for nearly an hour.

Police-Constable William Carter said that he saw a man 'dressed like the Bishop of Peterborough' with a young woman on the 15th March the previous year. According to the Constable, they went into the Grand Hotel, stayed there for about an hour, and then walked to the Bull Hotel.

Alice Blisset, an employee of the Grand Hotel, said that she remembered that a clergyman and a woman 'came in one evening for a hot bath'.

Excitement mounted when Douglas Hogg produced an unexpected witness. The Vicar of Stanground, a village two

miles to the south-west of Peterborough, told how he had seen
a clergyman in his church, with a young woman, at the time
of the Diocesan Conference at Peterborough in March 1920.
Clergymen very rarely came to his church, he said, and he
had written to the Bishop about it that February.

'Will you look round?' Hogg asked. 'Do you recognise
your visitor as being in court?'

'I see the Archdeacon sitting five persons from my right,'
came the reply.

Mrs Baker, the wife of a Lincoln bank manager who knew
Archdeacon Wakeford very well by sight, said that she saw
him standing on the platform at Peterborough Station at 1.30
p.m. on March 16th 1920. She remembered the date and
time very well indeed because she had been accompanying
the body of her mother from Bournemouth to Grimsby. As
the train had entered the station she had seen the Archdeacon
on the platform. She did not speak to him, but she was 'sure it
was he'.

Canon Morse, Vicar of Peterborough, related how he had
met Mr Worthington at the Bishop's Palace on May 31st
1920, had subsequently received two letters from
Worthington and had then gone to the Bull Hotel to examine
the visitors' book.

Douglas Hogg's next witness was a pedantic man with a
large, domed forehead and pince-nez spectacles. Mr Charles
Mitchell, Fellow of the Institute of Chemistry and member of
the Society of Public Analysts, was a handwriting expert. He
gave his professional opinion on the second entry in the hotel
register ('J. Wakeford, the Precincts, Lincoln' and 'M.
Wakeford'): 'there was nothing to show that they were
written at different dates, but it was not possible to state
positively that they were written at the same time'.

The Lord Chancellor said that this answer led to nothing.

The next witness was William Shuckburgh Swayne, Bishop
of Lincoln. His evidence flowed like honey after the faltering
utterances of the lay witnesses. In mellow clerical tones, the

court was told that the Bishop had not held any meeting of archdeacons on the Saturday after Good Friday 1920, neither had he ever contemplated doing so, or ever instructed anyone to ask Archdeacon Wakeford to call at the Palace on that day.

Edward Carson discovered that his Lordship was unaware that Wakeford had preached in the Cathedral on Palm Sunday, March 28th.

'You were not there?' Carson asked in some surprise.

'I was there in the evening of that Sunday.'

'Do you know that the Archdeacon went on that Sunday to stay in London with Archdeacon Bevan?'

'I understood so.'

'And that he was there on Good Friday when he came back?'

'I believe so.'

'And that it was contemplated that there would be a meeting of archdeacons?'

'No.'

'It was contemplated?'

'It came off on the Tuesday.'

'It had not come off by the time he left on the Sunday?'

'No.'

'So that when he went away he might have anticipated that there would be a meeting of the archdeacons?'

'I think that would be very unlikely: it was probably settled.'

'I want to know what you did. What did you do on the Saturday?' Carson enquired in an offhand manner.

'I played golf,' came the reply, and the four bishops on the bench laughed.

Bishop Swayne said that on Easter Eve he was in his Palace and, in reply to Edward Carson, reaffirmed that Archdeacon Wakeford had not called on him.

'Are you certain?'

'Yes; I can give you the reason why.'

'We will call our own evidence,' Carson said.

Douglas Hogg interrupted. 'What was the reason?'

'I discussed this matter, before it came before me with Mrs Wakeford...'

'I object,' snapped Carson. And on that cryptic note the Bishop's cross-examination ended.

A Mr Curlew, the new manager of the Bull Hotel, then appeared. He said that he had not been able to find any books relating to Pugh's management, other than those which had already been produced in evidence, and admitted to Edward Carson that there had been a 'general upheaval' when he had taken over the Bull in which 'some staff gave notice and some had to go'.

Curlew was the final prosecution witness to stand at the plain wooden lectern before lords Buckmaster, Dunedin, Shaw and Birkenhead. Hogg had amassed a formidable body of evidence implicating John Wakeford in an affair with a young woman at Peterborough the previous year. It was now the task of Edward Carson, in his last act of advocacy, to demolish that evidence.

9

IN THE BALANCE

'No counsel, however long he has been at the Bar, can fail to recognise that this is a case of unusual responsibility. Archdeacon Wakeford is an exceptional man. There are few men who have been harder workers in the cause of Christianity, to which he has professed himself to be devoted all his life. In the service of his Church he has been a living example and a foe to the hypocrisy which on all hands the Church abhors. The Archdeacon was born in 1859, ordained in 1884 and married in 1893 to a lady of whose brother I shall have something to say.'

These were Carson's opening words in the case for the defence of John Wakeford.

He described how his client had become Archdeacon in 1913, had lectured in the universities of London, Liverpool and Durham, in the United States and Canada, and was the author of twenty-four books of theology and devotion. No one in England was better known as a preacher. Yet the allegation was *not* that 'this Archdeacon in some underhand and illicit manner, concealing his identity and leading a double life, is guilty of adultery, but that in broad daylight, without concealment, in the neighbouring diocese to his own, went in clerical garb with a young woman who was not his wife and openly stayed with her at an hotel on two occasions.'

'If the case for the prosecution is true,' Carson said, 'then there can be no other explanation except that the Archdeacon is mad and nobody has ever made that suggestion.'

On the following day, the fourth of the appeal, Downing Street was jammed with people. The *Daily Express* reporter described the scene:

> Every inch of accommodation within the chamber was taken by the public, so great was the interest to hear the Archdeacon on his defence. The ushers — they wear evening dress in the Privy Council Court — achieved what seemed to be impossible by squeezing two people where normally one should stand. Fashionably dressed women, in heavy furs and winter cloaks, were present in great numbers. They did not mind the discomfort of the crush and the hours of standing so long as they could gaze and listen. The 'reserved enclosure' — the special seats behind the judges — were all taken. Lady Birkenhead, wife of the Lord Chancellor, was among those in court.

Squashed in at the back of the court was C.T. Moore, his grizzled head surrounded by ladies' hats.

Archdeacon Wakeford came to the witness stand, his mobile, expressive face heavily lined, revealing the strain of the past weeks. He detached his watch from its chain — as he always did before preaching — and placed it carefully on the rail to one side. Beside it he arranged his glasses, sermon note-book and leather brief-case. Then he looked down with clear blue eyes at the four lords of appeal.

Sir Marlay Samson, who had taken over from Carson, commenced the questioning. 'In the work of preparation of sermons what has been your custom?'

'It has been my custom to find some great church or

cathedral to which I might retire, and there I have made notes of the sermons. I have also walked by myself long distances in the country.'

Wakeford spoke as he did in the pulpit, emphasising his replies with grave, deliberate, almost theatrical gestures. There was total silence in the pauses between questions. The four bishops listened in rapt attention, the Bishop of London scarcely moved his gaze from Wakeford's face. C.T. Moore stared fixedly at the Archdeacon's back. Lord Birkenhead, his smooth hair gleaming, leaned back in his William and Mary chair, regarding Wakeford with sombre brown eyes.

Gradually, Samson extracted Wakeford's version of his visit to Peterborough. 'With what intention did you go to Peterborough?'

'That I might prepare my sermons and have a free day by myself in church. It was a place where I could have a walk and get back next day.'

Wakeford said that he had stayed at the Bull before, in 1912 and 1914, and knew Peterborough well. He had arrived at the hotel shortly after eight o'clock on the night of the 14th March. The hotel was very full and Pugh had told him that there was only one room available, a double-bedded one, which he took, and he signed the hotel register 'J. Wakeford, Precincts, Lincoln'. The book had never been brought to his room and no one had been with him at *any* time while he was in the hotel. There was no truth in Mrs Willcocks's evidence. He had dined that night in the public dining-room, at about twenty past eight, and afterwards had gone directly to bed, wearing a nightshirt. He never wore pyjamas, 'except when he was in France'.

In a full resonant voice, Wakeford related the events of the following day and his meeting with the girl in the Cathedral. After deciphering the memorial to the old sexton he had shown the girl the tombs of the two queens and afterwards taken her to a stationer's shop to help her buy a postcard. The card was no longer produced in colour, he was told, and the girl had bought a plain one. He had not seen her again.

Between March 14th and 16th he had not been in the streets of Peterborough with any woman. After luncheon on the 15th he had walked along the Great Western Road for two miles to Thorpe, and then on to Castor where he had taken tea, at the Fitzwilliam Arms. After visiting Castor church he had walked back in heavy rain to Peterborough, reaching the Bull Hotel at about half-past six. It was not true that Mrs Pugh had advised him to go to the public baths. When he was told that the heating apparatus in the hotel was out of order, he had asked for a fire to be made in his room so that he could dry himself.

In reply to Sir Marlay Samson, Wakeford said that he had dined at about seven o'clock. As he had no change of clothing he had gone straight to the public dining-room, and afterwards had dried his clothes in his room. At no time had he spoken to a police constable, nor had he bathed at the Grand Hotel.

Then Wakeford broke off and looked down at the Lord Chancellor. 'May I make a statement?'

Birkenhead nodded.

'I am an abstemious person,' Wakeford said. 'I have never drunk a bottle of champagne in my life.' He was troubled at the evidence that he had drunk champagne in the Bull Hotel: such an accusation was an aspersion on his character. Nor did he drink malt liquors *or* spirits.

Afterwards he continued with the events of the 16th March. He had breakfasted at twenty past eight and then gone to the post office for his mail, which he had arranged for his wife to forward to him, as he had not known where he would be staying in Peterborough. He had then cashed a cheque for £2 at the bank, returned to the hotel to pay his bill (which he 'paid within 2s 6d of £2 — more or less') and caught the 11.00 a.m. train to Lincoln. The parish clerk of Kirkstead, Mr Lanyman, had met the train at Kirkstead station at 12.50 p.m. to take some papers from him, and he had reached Lincoln 'a few minutes after 1.33 p.m'. He lunched at home

114

with his wife. It was not true that he had been at Mr Young's church at Stanground that morning — he had not been to that church for thirty years.

Then Wakeford turned to his visit to the Bull Hotel on Good Friday 1920. His wife had not accompanied him to London, when he preached at St Luke's, Chelsea, because that week she had been ill from nervous exhaustion and, what is more, his son had written to say that he would be coming home on leave from the army on Maundy Thursday. This being so, he had written to say that he would depart from London on Good Friday, spend the night at Peterborough and return to Lincoln on the Saturday. It was in any case necessary for him to do this, because of the meeting which had been called by the Bishop in Lincoln for that morning.

On his second visit, he had arrived at the Bull Hotel at about seven o'clock on Good Friday evening. There was no sign of either Tuplin or Sergeant King. He had written in the hotel book, as before: 'J. Wakeford, Precincts, Lincoln'. The words 'and wife' were, again, not written by him. He had eaten in the public dining-room at quarter to eight and had drunk a quarter of a bottle of claret as he had been 'greatly exhausted by the journey from London'. Then he went to his room. Next morning he had breakfasted in the private breakfast room.

'How did you come to go there on that day?' Birkenhead enquired.

Wakeford replied that there were only three guests in the hotel and they all ate in the private room that morning.

After breakfast, the waitress had brought him his bill. There was a mistake of a few shillings, which she rectified, and he gave her the change. The bill was for twelve or fifteen shillings, Wakeford recalled. He reached Lincoln at 10.41 a.m. and was met at the railway station by his son, John.

When he called at the Palace he was surprised to find that the Bishop was out and that there was to be no meeting that day.

★　　★　　★

On the fifth day of the appeal Sir Marlay Samson continued his examination; the Archdeacon's answers came without hesitation, in torrents of words and with growing confidence, as if he already sensed victory.

There was no truth whatever, Wakeford maintained, in Worthington's statement that he, Wakeford, had treated his wife in a disgraceful way, nor in the allegation that she had said so. Furthermore, contrary to what Worthington had said, he had always been on the best of terms with his father-in-law, who had died two years previously. The late Mr Worthington had always written to him in terms of great affection: the old man had written him six letters from his death bed. Furthermore, his wife and he were 'identified in every way'; they spent holidays together and had travelled abroad together. He had never opened her letters, although she was free to open any of his, and had done so. He was convinced that the whole case was a conspiracy against him.

'If you ask me who arranged it, I say, with great regret, my brother-in-law and Moore. If you ask what instruments they found, I say the readiest and ablest was Sergeant King. I say the others are more or less instruments half unwilling. I am not willing to blame all these people.'

Douglas Hogg cross-examined for an hour and a quarter, taking Wakeford once more through the events in Peterborough in March and April 1920.

'Your object,' Hogg commenced, 'in going to Peterborough on the first occasion was to have a quiet day in the churches?'

'Yes,' replied the Archdeacon, 'and on the roads.'

'Did you know the Diocesan Conference was going on?'

'I did.'

'Could you not have had a quiet day in the churches at Lincoln?'

116

'I might have had a quiet day, but the churches there were familiar to me, and I wanted something apart.'

Quietly, firmly and with great persistence Douglas Hogg plugged away, and Wakeford answered confidently. Only once did he come near to losing his temper, when Hogg pressed him about the bill during his first stay at the Bull.

'Your bill at the Bull was, you say, either £1 17s 6d or £2 2s 6d?'

'Yes, either way,' Wakeford responded.

'You had been there for two nights. You had, you say, two breakfasts, two dinners, one half-bottle of wine and a bath?'

'Yes.'

'Can you tell me how that made £2 or anything like it?'

'I cannot,' Wakeford admitted, 'I do not know the tariff.'

Then Birkenhead intervened. 'Were you aware what the charge for your room was to be?'

'I believe it was to be seven shillings,' Wakeford replied. 'The question to me was, "Will you take it as a double room?" I said "Yes", and I think they said it would be seven shillings.'

Douglas Hogg handed Wakeford the hotel account book so that the Archdeacon could refer to it.

Wakeford flared up. 'I want to see the original book from which the accounts were made up,' he retorted fiercely. '*This* book will give me very little information.'

Hogg persisted. 'Have you any explanation to give why you are charged for two breakfasts, two luncheons, two dinners on those days?'

'I have,' snapped Wakeford. 'They were charged up to support a statement that I had somebody with me when I had not.'

'You mean a deliberate falsification of the book?' Hogg asked.

'I am not going to be led into denunciation of anyone. I am on my defence, and I am making no accusation against anyone.'

Douglas Hogg emphasised that a large double-room had been reserved for the Archdeacon's second stay, at Easter.

'You put it that way,' Wakeford retorted. 'They had made an apology for the former room, which overlooked the stable yard. They said they had more pleasant rooms in front of the house, and gave me one of these. The house was empty.'

The Archdeacon denied that he had written the words 'and wife' in the hotel register: 'they strikingly resemble my writing, but they are not my writing'. The words 'M. Wakeford' must have been written in by someone before the next visitor arrived, four and a half hours later, at eleven o'clock.

'Your suggestion is that there was a conspiracy between Pugh, King, Worthington, Moore, Tuplin and an ignorant girl to write in a false entry in order to accuse you of this crime?' Hogg asked.

'I do not follow your statement,' said Wakeford. 'For instance, when you say that an ignorant girl was in conspiracy...' He paused, searched in his pocket and held up a coin to symbolise a bribe. 'No, poor child — a shilling. You asked who arranged it. I say, with much regret and great pain, my brother-in-law and Moore; the others were their poor instruments.'

Evelyn Wakeford followed her husband at the witness stand. To the society ladies in their smart furs she must have seemed a dowdy little thing — a typical clergyman's wife, dressed in a rough tweed costume with a small unfashionable hat. Looking pale and unwell, she was nevertheless calm and very much in control of herself. Although she had recently undergone surgery, Evelyn Wakeford refused Birkenhead's invitation to sit and gave her evidence standing up. In a clear, precise voice she spoke of the Rectory at Northlew and how she, her husband and family had stayed there regularly while her father was alive.

'What kind of confidence existed between you and your husband?' Sir Marlay asked.

'Absolute.'

'What was your practice regarding his letters if he were away from home?'

'I had absolute control of them. I opened them if necessary and would forward them to any address he gave me.'

Evelyn Wakeford said she had intended joining Wakeford in London for the whole or part of the week while he was preaching at Chelsea before Easter 1920. She had not done so because she had been feeling unwell: she had not told her husband this.

'So far as he was concerned, then,' asked Sir Marlay, 'would he be uncertain you were coming to London?'

'Absolutely uncertain.'

Later the questioning turned to the supposed differences between Evelyn Wakeford and her husband.

'Is there any truth in the statement that for seventeen or eighteen years you have told your brother of the "disgraceful" way in which your husband has behaved towards you?'

'No truth whatever,' came the reply.

'Is it true that on every occasion your brother has met you during the last fifteen years you have made statements about Evelyn Porter?'

'It is absolutely untrue.'

Evelyn Wakeford said that until the time of her father's death the relations between him and her husband had always been those of affection and trust.

'Have you ever complained to your brother of lightness of conduct on the part of your husband with any woman?' Birkenhead asked.

'Never,' came the implacable reply.

Mrs Wakeford then described the meeting with her brother at Burton-on-Trent in July and how he had threatened that if she had not slept at the Bull Hotel in March her husband would be charged with adultery. When her brother had suggested that the woman was Evelyn Porter, she had replied that this was *quite* impossible — Miss Porter was not of that

119

type. Worthington had replied that he had seen the hotel register and was sure about 'J. Wakeford' but not about the 'and wife'. When Evelyn Wakeford had seen the entries she was convinced that the 'and wife' was not in her husband's handwriting. Her husband invariably wore a nightshirt in bed and had only worn pyjamas in France in February 1919. These were not marked with his name and were still in a cupboard in a spare room at the Precentory.

Cross-examined by Douglas Hogg, Evelyn Wakeford admitted that her brother had written to her saying: 'You write as though I got up this tale. I did nothing of the kind. Think of all you have told me and mother about your husband.' She had replied, on the same day: 'You have been digging up graves which I had carefully bricked in and planted over.' Her complaints had never been of her husband's morality at any time, they were to do with personal problems of her own.

'I have never in my life had any suspicion of my husband's morality,' declared Mrs Wakeford.

She added that there had been a 'misunderstanding', and in her confusion she might have said, in a moment of annoyance, that she would have nothing more to do with her brother or her husband. Her complaint had never been of her husband's morality at any time: they were personal matters of her own.

'I was the offender in those days, not my husband,' she said with cold emphasis.

★   ★   ★

Next came a succession of witnesses, all confirming John Wakeford's testimony: his son, Lieutenant John Wakeford, R.E., who described how he met his father at the Great Northern Railway Station in Lincoln at 10.30 a.m. on April 1st 1920; and Fanny Drury, house-parlourmaid at the Precentory, who said that she had packed a nightshirt in the

Archdeacon's bag before he left Lincoln. His pyjamas had lain unused since 1919, she maintained. John Page, Verger, said that on the 15th March the Archdeacon had talked to a young woman in Peterborough Cathedral and had shown her the queens' tombs. The girl had left, by herself, and the Archdeacon had later talked to him in the Cathedral. Mrs Edith Roddies said that she had been cleaning brasses in Thorpe church, on the afternoon of the 15th March, and had seen the Archdeacon there — by himself. William Smith, licensee of Castor, swore that the Archdeacon had taken tea in the Fitzwilliam Arms, at four o'clock on the 15th March. Wakeford had been alone and stayed for about an hour.

Then Mary Blunden stepped nervously to the stand. A pretty, unpretentious young woman who had once been a barmaid, she looked frail with short, dark hair and a close-fitting hat; she related how she and her husband had arrived at Peterborough on the 15th March 1920. It was a very wet day and they had plodded round in teeming rain looking for hotel rooms. The Grand Hotel was one they visited; they had also enquired at a tea shop near the Bull Hotel. After waiting for two hours in the Bull they were given rooms and had dined at about half past eight she thought.

'Do you remember anything happening while you were in the dining-room?' Sir Marlay enquired.

'Yes, my husband asked me to take my hand off the table because I was not wearing my wedding ring.'

Later, Marlay Samson asked the witness what she had been wearing that day in Peterborough.

'A dark costume, dark furs and a dark velour hat.'

'What is velour?' Lord Buckmaster asked.

'Perhaps the witness can tell,' said Sir Marlay. 'I cannot tell.'

'A dark felt,' came the reply.

'Did you notice anyone in particular in the dining-room?' Marlay resumed.

'I noticed a man in clerical attire. He wore knee breeches.

121

He was alone, sitting at a table on the right-hand side of the fireplace.'

Mary Blunden was now deathly pale. She paused and then slumped forward in a faint. Lord Dunedin quickly produced smelling salts and Mrs Blunden was revived.

Douglas Hogg cross-examined her gently concerning her long wait in the hotel lobby, when, she said, she had not seen the Archdeacon.

Edmund Blunden confirmed his wife's evidence. She had been ill for a long time, he explained, and her fingers were too thin to wear a wedding ring. There was a brief murmur of laughter as the poet recalled the words that he spoke to his wife as they had sat at their table in the gloomy hotel dining room: 'Mary, take your hands off the table or they will throw you out of the place.'

★ ★ ★

The sixth day of the appeal commenced with a stir of excitement as Douglas Hogg was given leave to produce an unexpected witness: a stocky, dark-haired man in morning clothes. Harold Osborne was a hide and wool buyer from Worcester. In a quiet but emphatic voice, he told the court that he and his wife had been at the Bull Hotel on the 14th March 1920. They had gone to Peterborough for the weekend to visit Mr Osborne's mother and had returned to the hotel at 9.30 p.m. on the Sunday evening. Osborne and his wife were very thirsty and had been shown upstairs to 'a small room marked "private" ' to take tea. There they found an elderly clergyman sitting with a young woman at a table near a french window.

'Would you know that clergyman again?' asked Douglas Hogg.

'I should.'

'Do you see him now in court?'

Slowly, Osborne looked round the crowded courtroom and

122

deliberately raised his arm to point at Archdeacon Wakeford.

'That is the man.'

Wakeford — eyes cast down and half a smile on his lips — sat apparently indifferent to this dreadful blow from the dark.

Osborne went on to relate that his wife had gone to fetch a cake. While she was doing so, the young woman had got up from the table and sat near the fire, while the Archdeacon 'talked to a young man who was interested in motor-cycles'. Later, the woman had rejoined the Archdeacon and they left the room together.

On the following morning the Osbornes had breakfasted in the small private room. There they saw Archdeacon Wakeford and the young woman sitting at the table near the french windows with Mr and Mrs Pugh. According to Osborne, Wakeford and the woman had spoken very quietly to each other and he could not hear what they said. Osborne claimed that he next saw the couple at luncheon on that day, Monday, in the downstairs dining-room.

Cross-examined by Sir Edward Carson, Osborne said that he remembered very clearly what he saw during his stay at the Bull Hotel. When he had first read about the proceedings of the Consistory Court, he did not pay much attention to it. Later, he had not wanted to be drawn into the matter: it was 'not a nice thing to be connected with'.

'Oh come, you are very squeamish,' Carson said amidst general laughter and calls for silence by Lord Birkenhead. 'When did you lose your squeamishness?'

'When reading the case this week,' Osborne answered. 'I then telegraphed to Mr Hogg.'

Mrs Osborne corroborated her husband's evidence: the clergyman's companion had been 'pale, dark and of slight stature'.

'I only saw her side face. I should say she would be about thirty; anyway, she was quite young.'

Under cross-examination Mrs Osborne admitted that she had been in court while her husband gave evidence.

'Has your husband a very wonderful memory?' Carson enquired.

'Yes.'

'A really unusual memory?'

'No, a good memory. I always rely on him to remember things for me.'

'Did you rely on him to remember the evidence for you?'

'Oh, no,' Mrs Osborne protested, flustered.

★   ★   ★

The Bishop of Lichfield testified on Wakeford's behalf. 'While I understand that Archdeacon Wakeford has certain qualities which possibly make enemies, I think he is one of the cleanest living men I have known.' Canon Wooley of Lincoln said much the same: 'such a charge against such a man is monstrously absurd.'

There then appeared a succession of witnesses all testifying to the Archdeacon's version of the events in Peterborough between the 14th and 16th March 1920.

The manageress of the Grand Hotel said that there was no record in the bath book of anyone bathing at her hotel on the 15th March. A horse coper from Huddersfield maintained that he had seen a clergyman 'wearing gaiters and that sort of thing' enter the public dining-room at the Bull Hotel sometime between 6.00 and 9.00 p.m. on the 15th March. He now identified him as Archdeacon Wakeford. There had been no one with the Archdeacon and he had noticed no wine on his table.

A farmer from Orton, near Sheffield, said that he too had dined in the public dining-room on the 15th March and had seen Wakeford there. There was no woman with him. He had also encountered the Archdeacon — by himself — on the landing on the following morning and they had said 'good morning' to each other.

A Mr Appleby, of Stafford, testified that he had seen

124

Archdeacon Wakeford in the public dining-room on the evening of the 15th March and at breakfast the following morning. He had been alone on both occasions. David Thomas, of Hereford, corroborated Appleby's evidence, as did a scout master from Kettering, who said that he saw the Archdeacon sitting by himself at a table on the right-hand side of the fireplace at breakfast on the 15th March. Another horse breeder and his friend, and a veterinary surgeon from Market Drayton, had also seen the Archdeacon, alone, in the public dining-room on that morning and on the following one.

Excitement mounted in the court when it was Evelyn Porter's turn to be called. Before she entered, Lord Birkenhead turned to Douglas Hogg.

'I should like to know, is it any part of your case to make any aspersion upon the reputation or chastity of this lady?'

'It is not,' Hogg replied.

Birkenhead then turned to Edward Carson. 'What is the nature of the evidence which the witness is about to give?'

Carson replied that he was going to contend that there had been a persistent attempt by the Archdeacon's accusers to make a case against the witness. It rested on the alleged identification of her by Mr and Mrs Pugh at the Marlborough Street Police Court. Also Miss Porter should have the opportunity of refuting the words spoken and written by the Reverend Herbert Worthington coupling her name with that of the Archdeacon.

Their lordships consulted; Birkenhead gave their decision. They would hear Miss Porter's evidence, but only in so far as it might bear upon the accuracy of statements made by the Pughs.

Evelyn Porter entered the court, a slight figure with a bright, attractive complexion, her dark hair partly hidden under a brown straw hat. She was wearing a long-skirted, brown costume over a thick, grey, woollen jersey. Her resemblance to Evelyn Wakeford was uncanny.

Evelyn Porter described to Edward Carson how the Bishop

of Lincoln's solicitor had appeared in her room at the police court with a woman in tow. 'Mr Lee said to me "have you seen this woman before?"' Miss Porter said she thought the solicitor was speaking to the woman and had remained silent. Lee repeated his question. 'Oh, I see, you are speaking to me,' she had said and looked at the woman. 'I have to my knowledge never seen her in my life.' The solicitor had then turned to his companion. 'Have you seen this woman before?' The woman, whom she later learned was Mrs Pugh, said 'yes', tossed her head and walked out of the room with Mr Lee.

Evelyn Porter's evidence was the last that was given in the Wakeford appeal.

★ ★ ★

On the following Monday morning, Downing Street was again packed with a jostling crowd. They rushed forward when the oak doors of the courtroom were opened. Women, journalists and elderly clergymen struggled fiercely to get in. The *Daily Express* reporter was shocked. 'It was a scene frankly disgraceful. The well-dressed women acted like barbarians. They tore at each others' garments, they elbowed, they butted, they kicked, and indeed improved on every trick of unfair scragging — there is no other word for it — learned in the hard campaigning of bargain sales.'

Court officials and policemen were overwhelmed and only by sheer force managed to shut the doors. There was a babble of shrill voices outside and noisy battering at the solid oak. Inside, the crowd was packed so tightly that it swayed to and fro as frenzied women — their hats awry, clothing in disarray — strained for fleeting glimpses of Archdeacon Wakeford.

Edward Carson's masterly closing speech was the last he would ever make as an advocate. He dominated the courtroom with the force of his personality and the power of his eloquence. Methodically, he examined every scrap of evidence that turned the scales for Wakeford. Every discrepancy in the prosecution evidence was exposed, every inconsistency emphasised as Carson hammered home his client's innocence. He made no bones about where he thought the real guilt lay.

'I emphatically say the origin of this case is Moore, the clergyman. Moore, who resented the part the Archdeacon had played in his prosecution, and the fact that the Archdeacon had got the Bishop to re-open the church at Kirkstead. Moore was the first man that Worthington went to when the question was raised that Archdeacon Wakeford had stayed at an hotel with a woman who was not his wife.'

The Archdeacon had sworn that he left the Bull Hotel on the Tuesday morning of his first visit to Peterborough. There was no reason, Carson argued, why their lordships should not believe the evidence of Mrs Wakeford that he had lunched at home that day, despite the testimony of the Reverend Mr Young and Mrs Baker. The evidence of Mr Young was entirely unsatisfactory.

As for the evidence of the Osbornes, who swore they saw the Archdeacon having a meal with a lady in the hotel: 'Can you attach the slightest importance to their evidence? Is it not perfectly plain that Mr Osborne has come forward to profess to recollection which it would be impossible for any man to have?'

Furthermore, the fact that the Archdeacon had dined in the public room at the Bull on the 14th March was not one that could be mistaken. All the guests who had testified that the Archdeacon had dined on that day had come from different parts of England: if their evidence were true it followed that the evidence of the Pughs could not be relied upon. And that put an end to the case, Carson maintained.

Finally, there was the matter of the mystery woman of the Bull Hotel, Peterborough.

'Where is this woman?' asked Sir Edward. 'Where is the

real evidence of the woman having been present at the hotel at all? Where did he pick this woman up? Did nobody see her? Did he pick her up en route for Peterborough? Was she a Peterborough prostitute, or a Peterborough woman lending herself to immorality, and, if so, how was it she was never traced by the police? What kind of woman would lend herself to this? She goes to a hotel without luggage, without even a nightdress, but it is not possible to think that the Archdeacon was so far gone in immorality and lowness that he took with him a woman without having a nightdress, or apparel that was necessary among any class of people ordinarily clean and decent.

'That woman is a myth,' Carson declared. 'She is an invention in this case. She does not exist. If she existed no man would have the moral courage to come here day after day with the thought that at any moment that woman might send a telegram or come into court to confront the Archdeacon as a perjurer, bringing disgrace on himself and his office.'

This last superb act of advocacy won even the admiration of Hogg's junior, William Stable: 'Carson's performance was a tour de force: he had not a card in his hand but he decided to dominate the whole proceedings.' Stable judged that the case was once more running strongly against the prosecution. 'Wakeford felt we were a routed army: it was the Bishop who was in the dock, his supporters were malicious men bent on the destruction of a great Christian prelate. You could feel the hostility of the court.'

★   ★   ★

Such was the atmosphere when Douglas Hogg rose to his feet after the luncheon interval. There had been another unseemly scramble for places when the doors were re-opened to the public, but there was total silence in the jammed courtroom as Hogg commenced his closing speech. His approach was in

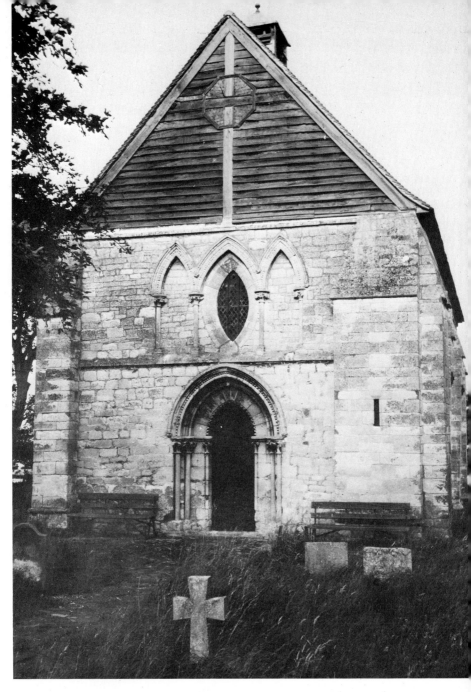

14 Kirkstead Church

15 *Above* Charles Moore, Rector of Appleby Magna, in middle age

16 *Left* Herbert Worthington, Rector of Netherseal, ca 1930

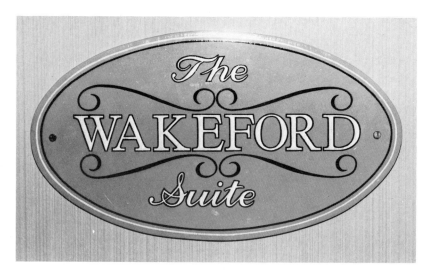

17 Sign outside Room 15 at the Bull Hotel in the present day

18 The Bull Hotel, Peterborough, at the turn of the century

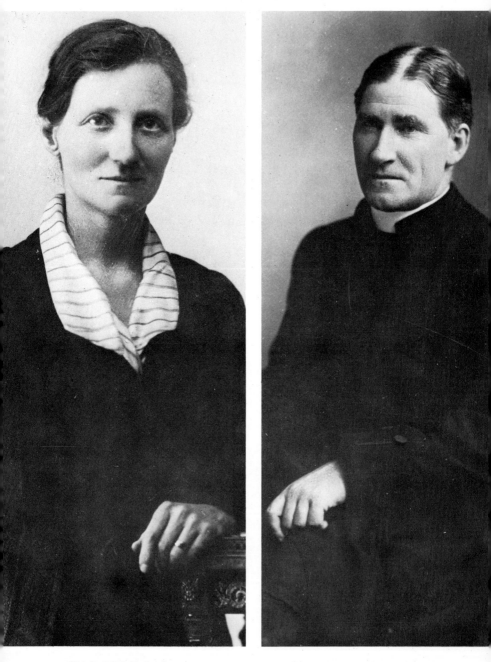

19 Evelyn Wakeford, 1921   20 John Wakeford, 1921

complete contrast to Carson's. There was no rhetoric, no emotion. Quietly, step by step, Hogg examined the evidence. His analysis was impressive by its very coolness and moderation.

Hogg scoffed at the idea of a conspiracy: it was an impossibility. There had been no reason at all for the Archdeacon going to Peterborough on the 14th March except the one that was alleged. Wakeford's explanation for booking a double room 'would not do'. His real name and address was 'Archdeacon John Wakeford, The Precentory, Lincoln', yet he had written in an illegible fashion 'J. Wakeford, Precincts, Lincoln'. Then there were the Pughs, Caroll, Willcocks, Young and Mr and Mrs Osborne, all of whom had said that the Archdeacon stayed at the Bull Hotel with a lady; the only alternative explanation was that they were all committing perjury. The defence had offered no explanation for the visit to the tapestry school.

Hogg then turned to the alleged chance encounter with the girl in the Cathedral. 'There are obvious reasons why the woman of the Bull Hotel should not come forward. There can be no reason why this girl should not have come forward *if* she existed. If there were such a girl, she would have been found by this time, *unless* she were the woman with the Archdeacon, and in that case there is every reason why she should not be forthcoming.'

'It was said,' Hogg continued, 'that the police were all parties to this vast conspiracy.' Yet on the evening of the 15th March the police themselves had recorded that the Archdeacon was staying at the hotel with a woman. They had that from Canon Morse and the Dean of Peterborough, and that was the strongest possible evidence that the presence of the woman was not an afterthought.

Hogg continued through the afternoon, quietly building his case, analysing the evidence, undermining Carson's arguments with cool logic, adroitly deflecting the questions which were interjected with increasing frequency by the four law lords, who seemed perplexed by much of the evidence against Wakeford, and especially by Worthington's and Moore's part in obtaining it.

'It is strange,' Birkenhead said, 'that Worthington did not approach his sister in the first instance, or communicate with the Archdeacon.'

Hogg explained that while Worthington was not un-friendly, he was not on intimate terms with his brother-in-law.

'He selected a sleuth hound,' Birkenhead retorted.

'And he was a man who would leave no stone unturned to bring this charge home to the Archdeacon,' added Lord Buckmaster.

Birkenhead asked what counsel had to say about the evidence of the name on Wakeford's pyjamas.

'It is puzzling to know what the real explanation of that is,' Hogg admitted lamely. 'It is possible that the Pughs might have been mistaken and seen the name on someone else's garments.'

The Lord Chancellor said that this could not be enter-tained.

'As regards the evidence of the Archdeacon's statement, "You must be wise," do you suggest that Mrs Willcocks was a witness of truth?', Birkenhead demanded.

'It is possible that it might have happened,' Hogg countered.

'There is this great difficulty,' Birkenhead continued. 'One must be careful not to exaggerate a statement made to Agar, who was selected by Moore as the instrument for taking these statements.'

'People of that type *are* apt to exaggerate,' Hogg admitted. 'Mr and Mrs Blunden's explanation of the ring incident is probably the true one.'

In his closing remarks, Hogg stressed the weight of the combined evidence of the hotel witnesses, the police, the outside witnesses and that of the account books. 'In my submission,' he concluded, 'when all these facts are taken into account, there is no possible conclusion which can be reasonably arrived at on the facts of this case except that the Archdeacon has been proved guilty of the charge.'

Despite the frailty of some of the evidence and the apparent scepticism of Birkenhead, William Stable felt that Hogg had presented a convincing case. 'He stripped the defence of all the fustian in which Carson had arranged it and exposed it as being non-existent. Slowly, the tide ebbed; the quiet logical build-up of every known fact in its appropriate place presented a complete picture, it was unanswerable.'

Young Stable was, in fact, bursting with admiration for his senior's performance. 'I think Lord Birkenhead struggled to the last but was eventually convinced. It was a magnificent example of a great general, whose army had been routed, re-organising the troops and snatching victory from disaster.'

But Stable's euphoria was premature: Lord Birkenhead was not convinced of Wakeford's guilt.

10
FINAL JUDGMENT

Birkenhead's judgment on the Wakeford case was said to be
the most brilliant of his life; it was certainly the one which
caused him most anguish. His wife said that he suffered
'mental agony' during the seven days that he worked on the
evidence. He was still awake, and fully dressed, an hour
before dawn on the showery April morning when he was due
to give judgment. He woke his wife at 4 a.m., his face
haggard, a large magnifying glass clenched in his powerful
hand, to seek her opinion on a photograph of Wakeford's
entry in the hotel register.

It was undoubtedly an extremely difficult case; the conflict
of evidence was complex and extreme. But there was more to
it than that, for Lady Birkenhead said that her husband
'wanted to believe that Archdeacon Wakeford was innocent'.
It may have been, as William Stable suspected, that as a
Liverpool man of modest beginnings and driving ambition
Birkenhead felt a strong affinity with Wakeford and may have
believed that it would have been wiser for the Bishop of
Lincoln to have turned a blind eye to what was, after all, only
a human frailty — a frailty he himself shared, for at the time

'F.E.' was engaged in a passionate affair with a beautiful, golden-headed girl.

Mona Dunn was the daughter of Sir James Dunn, a Canadian financier and boyhood friend of Lord Beaverbrook. She attended the same finishing school as Birkenhead's daughter. 'F.E.' met her in Paris at the time of the Peace Conference in 1919, when she was seventeen; Mona Dunn was besotted with Birkenhead and sometime in the next year they became lovers. This could never have shaken Birkenhead's legal impartiality, but it must have coloured his emotions as he struggled to decide whether the Archdeacon of Stow had taken a young woman to the Bull Hotel at Peterborough.

Birkenhead delivered his judgment in the crowded chamber of the Privy Council on the morning of the 26th April 1921. There was only a brief moment of suspense after Birkenhead took his place at the long table with the lords Buckmaster, Dunedin and Shaw, Birkenhead announced:

'Their lordships are of the opinion that this appeal fails.'

John Wakeford, sitting with his daughter at his side, closed his eyes briefly. To one spectator, 'it was as though all his courage and nerve had been summoned from within him to meet that one moment bravely. That curious half-whimsical expression, which is so characteristic of the man, remained stamped upon his face...His young daughter, who was his only companion, was obviously distressed. Her face went pale to the lips and her eyes kept turning towards her father, appealing, wondering, searching in their look.'

The hard-bitten reporter of the *Daily Express* was moved. 'What ever else may be said of John Wakeford, Archdeacon of Stow, he can meet adversity with a brave front.'

Wakeford scarcely changed his position during the hour and three quarters it took the Lord Chancellor to read the court's decision. Occasionally, he leaned forward to catch a special reference to himself. Now and again, he flushed and sometimes plucked at his cuffs or fiddled with the buttons of his frock coat as Birkenhead ploughed through page after page of closely reasoned argument.

In his preamble, Birkenhead outlined the circumstances of the appeal, and the few precedents for such proceedings under the Clergy Discipline Act of 1892, before detailing the Archdeacon's version of events in Peterborough the previous year. One paragraph in particular contained the crux of the matter:

> The narrative of the Appellant's movements during the material period depends almost entirely upon his own statement, which is corroborated in certain particulars by the statements of others; but, being essentially the product of one mind, and that the mind of a man of observation and intelligence, on matters within his own knowledge, it is complete and consistent with itself, though on many details, as well as on the main issue, whether he was alone or in company, it necessarily differs from the evidence given by the witnesses for the prosecution. This latter evidence, on the other hand, is a mosaic of statements made by a great number of persons, each of whom can only speak to particular moments of time or particular instances. It does not fit together so as in all respects to form a complete picture, nor is it always consistent with itself.

Birkenhead conceded that there was common ground between the prosecution and the appellant concerning Wakeford's visit to Peterborough Cathedral and his walk to Thorpe and Castor on the afternoon of the 15th March, although there was disagreement about the times and durations of these events. On all other points there was conflict: none more so than with the hotel witnesses and the evidence of the police. There was also disagreement about the alleged visit, for about an hour, to the tapestry school with a young woman, which Wakeford denied, late on the morning of the 15th. Birkenhead emphasised here that the witness,

Miss Weston, could not fix the date of the visit except by the recollection that it occurred during a heavy snow storm at a time when the school was at work on a banner.

The Lord Chancellor acknowledged that there were grave inconsistencies between the evidence of the hotel witnesses, notably between Pugh and Tuplin concerning their identification of the Archdeacon, and a lack of candour on the part of the police and even positive mis-statement.

> This was not a case which the police were called upon to pursue when their suspicions had been allayed, as, by all accounts, they were on the evening of 15th March. If and so far as the police are concerned in any such affair, they are bound to a full disclosure of every motive, and it is a disquieting circumstance that they should, in this case, give a misleading explanation of their actions. The defence explain their conduct as part of a conspiracy to ruin the Appellant, and it is part of the unsatisfactory nature of the explanations offered to the Consistory Court which compels their Lordships critically to examine this hypothesis.

But first Birkenhead dealt with other disturbing conflicts of evidence. There was, for example, the matter of Wakeford's luncheon on the 16th March. The Pughs swore that he had lunched in the grill room of the hotel on that day, evidence which was flatly contradicted by that of Mr Lanyman, the Kirkstead parish clerk, and by Mrs Wakeford, who said that her husband took lunch with her in Lincoln. However, their lordships had been impressed by the independent evidence of the Vicar of Stanground, that Wakeford had been in his church with a woman at about eleven o'clock and by Mrs Baker's alleged sighting of the Archdeacon at Peterborough station at half past one.

Against the evidence of the Blundens, which their lordships accepted, and that of the other guests who saw Wakeford alone at the Bull Hotel, Birkenhead set that of Mr Osborne, the hide and wool buyer, and his wife. Their lordships were strongly swayed by their testimony:

> The evidence of Osborne and his wife is impressive. He, in particular, is a man of considerable intelligence and he was not shaken in cross-examination. Their evidence was offered spontaneously though, as it has been said, at the eleventh hour...Whatever observation may be made on this, it does not appear to their lordships incredible that Mr Osborne and his wife should have shrunk from taking part in the proceedings. It is indisputable that they stayed at the Bull Hotel during the material period. Their names and amounts debited to them appear in the tabular book. The counterfoil receipt given to them appears in the book of pink slips. On the other hand, their names do not appear in the visitors' book, and it is probably owing to this fact that neither side got into communication with them. If the theory of conspiracy be adopted, it is certain that the Osbornes have no connection with the plot. Their evidence can be set aside only upon the ground of mistake and, difficult as it is to explain away the evidence of Mr Young of Stanground and Mrs Baker upon the hypothesis of mistake, the difficulty of disposing of the evidence of Mr and Mrs Osborne appears to their lordships to be immensely greater.

Birkenhead next turned to Moore and Worthington and the contention by the defence that they had conspired to ruin Wakeford.

> As regards Moore, it should be said at once that his employment of a retired policeman, who had had what Worthington calls the good sense to marry his cook, to undertake unofficial inquiries into a matter with which he had little obvious concern is one of the least agreeable features of a painful case, and their lordships have most

136

scrupulously examined the result of inquiries so conducted, which can only be accepted with much reserve.

But animus in Worthington and bitterness on the part of Moore, coupled with such conduct as has last been described, fall far short of establishing the case sought to be made on behalf of the Appellant, or of destroying the formidable body of evidence arrayed against him.

The evidence showed, Birkenhead said, that if there was conspiracy it would have had to be made as early as the 15th March.

If the theory of conspiracy is pinned down to so early a date, its impossibility becomes apparent. When the Appellant left Lincoln on the evening of the 14th he had told his wife, and so far as we know no other person, that he was going to Peterborough, but he did not tell her that he was going to stay at The Bull. Indeed, he only made up his mind to do so when the train arrived. He had last stayed at Peterborough in 1918. He then slept at The Angel. He had stayed at The Bull twice — in 1912 and 1914. Let it be assumed that Moore and Worthington were waiting eagerly for an opportunity to trap the Appellant. Why should they have selected Peterborough to be the stage for their machination? Let it be assumed that King was their willing instrument in this daring and wicked plan. How did it come about that he had been either already selected and corrupted for the purpose before the Appellant went to Peterborough at all, on the mere chance that he might go there some day, or that Moore and Worthington from their respective vicarages of Appleby Magna and Netherseal procured his services in the hours that elapsed between Sunday evening and Monday afternoon? Let it be assumed again that the plot had been framed and set in motion. By what amazing coincidence did it come about that the

Appellant should have selected on this occasion the one hotel in Peterborough whose landlord was ready to be corrupted, able to carry with him into this maze of slander and perjury his wife and his servants, and zealous to commence a systematic course of forgery in support of the plan?

With this lucid paragraph, Birkenhead disposed of the possibility of conspiracy. The remainder of the judgment drove home their lordships' conviction of Wakeford's guilt. It was unreasonable to expect the prosecution to prove its case with every witness or to extract from them greater intelligence or more exact powers of memory than would normally be expected of such persons. As to the defence's submission of the extreme improbability of the charge brought against someone of such previous good character, it could have been part of an audacious plan by Wakeford to escape detection by flaunting his name and distinctive costume in a neighbouring cathedral town although it was 'difficult indeed to associate simplicity so absolute with a course so perilous'.

To Birkenhead and his peers, it was inconceivable that the girl in the Cathedral, if she was merely a chance companion, should not have come forward. She was evidently not an uneducated woman — certainly not illiterate — and it was impossible to imagine that she would not have seen newspaper accounts and photographs or heard gossip on the subject. Surely an innocent woman would not have been so callous as obstinately to hold her peace when a word from her would have cleared Wakeford?

There remained the matter of the visitors' book. The entry on the 14th March 1920 was: 'J. Wakeford and wife, 15, Precincts, Lincoln'. It was common ground that the words 'and wife' had been inserted with pencil by Pugh, most probably on the Monday, and that the remainder had been written by Wakeford. His name was badly written and Pugh had at first read it as 'Urthfold'. There was controversy as to whether the address was written at the same time, as claimed by the defence, or whether the words, 'Precincts, Lincoln', were added subsequently as claimed by Pugh and the police witnesses. To their lordships it appeared that the address had been written at another time, with a different pen, thus to a certain extent confirming Pugh's statement.

The April entry was:

J. Wakeford and wife 8 Precincts, Lincoln

M. Wakeford M.   8   ,,   ,,

According to the Archdeacon, he wrote *only* the words 'J. Wakeford, Precincts, Lincoln'; the room number, '8', was inserted by Pugh. Obviously if the Archdeacon had written 'J. Wakeford and wife' the case was at an end. But there were doubts. The form 'So and So *and wife*' was unusual for a man of Wakeford's social habits. He might have been expected to write 'Mr & Mrs Wakeford' or 'Archdeacon and Mrs Wakeford'. Furthermore, there was someone in the hotel who had already used this unusual form: Pugh had added 'and wife' to the March entry and used the same formula in the tabular book. In addition, there was no reason for the Archdeacon's alleged companion to have entered her name 'M. Wakeford M.' for, by so doing, she would have increased the chance of detection.

Immediately below the entry was the name of the next guest, put in not later than the following day. So 'M. Wakeford M.' must have been written by the alleged woman or — by some device — kept open until an opportunity occurred later for the hotel management to enter the disputed words. If this was the case, it was inconceivable that they would have been filled in while Wakeford was still in the hotel.

The writing of 'and wife' was indistinguishable from Wakeford's. The 'f' in 'wife' was very similar to that in 'Wakeford' of the 14th March; the dotting of the 'i' was characteristic and quite different from that in Pugh's earlier entry of these words in the visitors' book. Thus, if 'and wife' was a forgery it would have had to have been a very skilled one. And this Birkenhead considered improbable.

> 'Looking at the papers before them, their lordships, upon the evidence of their own eyes, have reached the conclusion that there can be no doubt upon the matter. If this was the only piece of evidence, their lordships, though without doubts in their own minds as to the authenticity of the writing, would not willingly rest their judgement on a single fact as to which error might be possible. For the reasons already given, their lordships feel that the hypothesis of such a conspiracy is utterly untenable. It follows that the writing in such circumstances furnishes overwhelming corroboration of the other evidence.'

This was the final blow. The Bishop's sentence would be enforced: 'That the Archdeacon be deprived of all his ecclesiastical promotion within the diocese of Lincoln, and especially the archdeaconry of Stow and of the canonry and the precentorship of Lincoln Cathedral, of the vicarage of Kirkstead, and of all the profits and benefits appertaining thereto, and of any other ecclesiastical promotions within the diocese of Lincoln.'

11
BOTTOMLEY
TO THE RESCUE

'I am still a priest,' Wakeford told jostling reporters ' — and I shall remain a priest.'

He was tired and dishevelled: he seemed to have aged dreadfully; his fleshy face was deeply lined and pallid beneath the broad brim of a shovel hat. Yet he was as defiant as ever. 'Circumstances have beaten me, but only for the time. My faith is unshaken. I know that I am innocent.'

The shock of defeat had been terrible and there was a final bitter necessity: the telegram to his wife in Lincoln to tell her the news. He wrote it himself in his neat hand: 'We have lost the case but you are yourself and I am content'.

That evening Wakeford returned to Lincoln and the wife who was too ill to share his ordeal: it would break her heart to leave their quiet home with its beautiful walled garden in the shadow of the Cathedral. There were the legal costs to face, and the sniggering of errand boys, and averted eyes in the Cathedral Close.

The morning newspapers were full of the case. *The Times* published a long leading article, scarcely concealing its incredulity at the Appeal Court verdict: 'many will approach a consideration of the evidence with the question in their minds whether a jury would have been entitled to find a verdict of "Guilty" on such testimony in a capital charge'. The writer was worried about the improbability of the offence, which made it almost necessary to 'contemplate madness in a man who, when he was bent on immorality, went in his clerical garments in the broad light of day with a woman to a large and crowded hotel in a cathedral town'.

'Add to that,' the article continued, 'the fact that eight witnesses, most of them farmers or horsebreeders who were staying at the Bull Hotel in March 1920, during a horse fair, all swore that they saw the Archdeacon alone in the public dining-room and alone in the public breakfast-room at the very times when the witnesses on the other side said that he was accompanied by a woman'.

The Times also devoted two whole pages to the Lord Chancellor's judgment, which it printed in full, 'so that members of the public may see on what evidence the decision is based'.

The other national dailies all had something to say about the Wakeford case, ranging from uneasy accounts of Birkenhead's judgment and stirring reports of Wakeford's defiance to outright approval of the judicial procedure and the verdict. For the *Daily Express*, 'the even hand of justice had been applied', while the *Daily News* drew comfort from the surprising fact that 'in this imperfect and difficult world so few good men go wrong'. The *Church Times* waded in with a leading article of outspoken satisfaction at the outcome of 'this sad and repulsive case'. There could be 'no shadow of doubt' that justice had been done. Wakeford was even berated for seeking justice. 'Knowing his guilt, Archdeacon Wakeford refused to admit it and to accept his punishment. If he had done so, we are sure Churchmen would have for him today no other feeling than that of sympathy and pity'. As it was, 'Mr' Wakeford had lost everything and 'to a sin detestable in itself had added betrayal of his friends' who were also condemned to 'the valley of humiliation with him who is condemned'.

But there were many who were not aware that they should be humiliated. One was the editor of the weekly magazine, *The Nation and the Athenaeum*, who if not exactly a friend was certainly a strong sympathiser. Edmund Blunden composed a vigorous leading article for the issue of the 30th April. He was convinced that there had been a conspiracy and dismissed the evidence against Wakeford as 'a bundle of frail or rotten sticks'. As for the three bishops, their assistance at the trial was worth 'no more than that of three sensible greengrocers': they were not required for purposes of justice and, at best, their presence was otiose.

In another column of the magazine, Blunden gave a vivid account of his arrival with Mary at the Bull Hotel on the drenching evening before the Horse Fair. He had not been impressed by Charles Pugh, a morose man whom Blunden had been unable to engage in conversation and who had 'tapped his teeth with a pencil as he moved in uncertain orbit from his office'.

He described his visit to Lincoln to provide evidence to Wakeford's solicitor before the trial; he had experienced at first hand the hostility which existed there against the Archdeacon.

He was dismayed by the arrangements for handling witnesses at the appeal trial, by the fact that Mrs Osborne had been allowed to sit in the court while her husband was giving evidence, by the herding of the witnesses into the same room where they were free to talk amongst themselves. Blunden had been impressed by the 'shire men' who had testified on Wakeford's behalf: 'witnesses of the best type, men from Hereford, from Yorkshire, from Louth, and elsewhere'. They too had had trouble with the Pughs' erratic book keeping and the make-shift arrangements at the Bull Hotel. One of the witnesses told Blunden that he had shared a room, next to Wakeford's, with a veterinary surgeon: he had worn pyjamas and the surgeon a nightshirt. Blunden had disliked, and was deeply suspicious of, the Osbornes who came so 'unaccountably late in the day' and by Mrs Osborne's evidence which was a 'mere corroboration' of her husband's.

'I for one,' wrote Blunden, 'cannot, after my connection with this case, see wherein lies the clinching proof of the Archdeacon's guilt.'

Blunden's outrage was echoed by his readers, and letters of protest poured into *The Nation and the Athenaeum*. Mary Blunden appealed for donations to cover Wakeford's legal expenses and a Canon Coop opened a fund in Liverpool.

★　　★　　★

Wakeford acquired some remarkable allies at this time. One of them was a friend of Birkenhead: a squat, grotesque little man with heavy sallow features and a predilection for champagne and kippers. Horatio Bottomley the swindler was approaching the end of his chequered career as politician, financier and newspaper baron, womaniser and patriot. By 1921 Bottomley's weekly newspaper *John Bull* was faltering; it had lost the force which it had built up during the war with its mixture of patriotic bombast and the 'Tommy and Jack' column devoted to the welfare of the brave lads in the trenches. Even the repeated drubbing of the scoundrel Frank Harris (formerly its theatre columnist) was losing much of its savour. Bottomley had spent £12,000 on a disabled German submarine, *Deutschland*, and this venture had ended in failure (with a disastrous explosion during its re-fit). Attempts to sell victory trophies, including busts of the editor moulded from the *Deutschland*'s metal, did not much appeal to the readers of *John Bull*.

Bottomley saw the Wakeford Case as a golden opportunity to revive the sagging fortunes of his journal. Here was grave injustice, spiced with suggestions of clerical promiscuity; the editor of *John Bull* knew only too well how to exploit that kind of thing.

Wakeford accepted Bottomley's offer of help. He may have done so even during the appeal itself, for in a statement to newspapermen immediately after the trial he used a phrase — to seek justice 'before the still greater Court of Public Opinion' — which could have come straight from Bottomley's mouth.

Bottomley launched his campaign in the issue of the 7th May 1921. '£1,000 REWARD FOR FINDING THE LADY', bawled the headline: 'THE ARCHDEACON WAKEFORD MYSTERY — "JOHN BULL'S" OFFER FOR PRODUCTION OF ESSENTIAL WITNESSES.'

The article did not presume, on purely legal grounds, 'to criticise the judgment of so august a tribunal as the Judicial Committee of the Privy Council' — far from it — but 'before the still greater court of public opinion other considerations hold'.

What worried *John Bull*, or its creator at least, was that when the matter came before the Consistory Court and the Judicial Committee *'the woman was out of it'*. And this Bottomly intended to rectify, to the benefit of British justice and the fortunes of his ailing newspaper.

Under the sub-heading, 'CHERCHEZ LA FEMME', the editor outlined his plan for a 'definite offer' of a reward of £1,000 for the production of 'the girl in the Cathedral'. A similar sum would also be paid to any woman who could prove that 'she stayed with Archdeacon Wakeford on the material dates at the Bull Hotel, Peterborough, in circumstances of such a nature as to justify the findings of the Judicial Committee'; her name would not be revealed, provided that she could prove her story to the editor's satisfaction.

Although Bottomley started the search for the missing lady, or ladies, it is very unlikely that he wrote the articles which, week after week, poured forth in *John Bull*; he was content to leave that to one of his underlings and only on the rarest occasions allowed it to interfere with his horse-racing and

THE 'JOHN BULL' PEN COUPON is on Page 14.

JOHN BULL

VOL. XXIX. No. 781.   SATURDAY, MAY 21, 1921   TWOPENCE.

[*Registered at the G.P.O. as a Newspaper.*]

Edited by HORATIO BOTTOMLEY

ON THE TRACK
of the WAKEFORD WOMAN

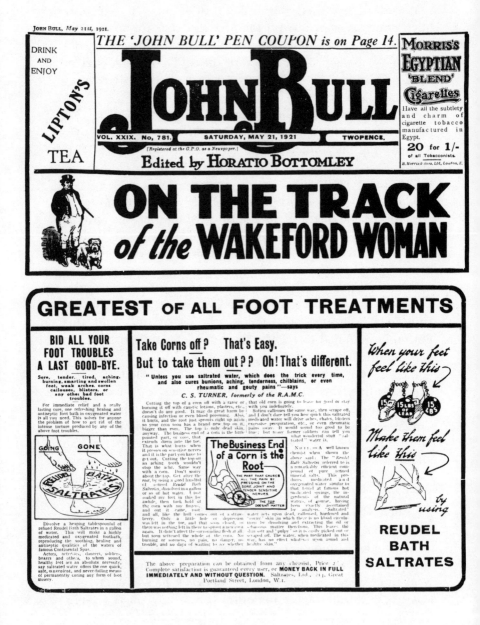

philandering. Most of Bottomley's articles were ghosted; he merely soled and heeled them with a few choice sentences, dashed off as the mood took him — at the race course, in his panelled office in King Street with its life-size bust of Bradlaugh on the oak mantelpiece or in the garden of his ugly, rambling mansion near Eastbourne.

The reward was increased the following week. '£2,000 TO FIND THE LADY', was sprawled across the front page beside the familiar stocky figure of John Bull, bulldog at heel, above a half-page advertisement for Cow and Gate baby food.

Excitement increased in the next issue with another front page banner headline: 'ON THE TRACK OF THE WAKEFORD WOMAN'. The editor's views were given in a double-page centre spread, the opening paragraph of which had the authentic Bottomley stamp:

I have made up my mind to deal, this week, in a more direct fashion than hitherto with the outstanding features of the Wakeford Drama, for the deeper I go into the case the more that I am satisfied that, in spite of the recent decision of the Judicial Committee of the Privy Council, it remains in the category of unsolved mysteries... I am happy to be able to inform my readers that, although at the moment of writing the reward of £2,000 has not been claimed, we appear to be on the track of the 'Missing Lady'. But before I indicate the result of our investigations, I want to say just a word or two from a personal standpoint upon the general aspects of this mysterious case. I realise that it is no light thing to impugn the judgement of so august a tribunal as the Judicial Committee of the Privy Council, or to question the soundness of a decision reached by a Bench composed of the most eminent Judges in the land. Nevertheless, I cannot unreservedly submit my judgement on a matter of this sort to any body of lawyers, however erudite and distinguished, and it very forcibly occurs to me that this is just one of those cases in which the opinion of the intelligent Man-in-the-Street may be as worthy of respect as that of the most eminent judicial personage whoever wore a wig. Of one thing, at any rate, I am perfectly certain in my own mind, and that is, that if Archdeacon Wakeford had been tried by a jury he would have been acquitted.

And Horatio Bottomley knew what he was writing about. Lacking any formal training in law, he had acquired a reputation of legal invincibility as a result of his successful court appearances and was generally known as 'the greatest lay lawyer in Britain'; certainly Birkenhead, who had been deeply engaged in some of Bottomley's affairs, had reason to respect his legal acumen.

The momentous news that the 'Girl in the Cathedral' had been found was revealed in the next issue of *John Bull*. Her name was not given, only that she was married to a Peterborough man and had taken lessons in painting and sketching. It was explained that 'without a doubt, she would have come forward earlier with an account of her meeting with a clergyman on the morning of 15th March 1920, only that her husband was at the time considerably worried over business matters, and unwilling, therefore, to incur the publicity inseparable from Court proceedings'.

A statement which had been signed by the girl was printed in full:

'I have special reasons for remembering Monday, March 15th. It was a wet day, and I went out for a walk after breakfast. My husband had left for business some time before, and I had arranged with him to meet him in the Cathedral Yard at about half-past ten. I went to the Cathedral and waited about — as I was rather early for the appointment. While waiting, I was having a good look at the building, and particularly at the little windows on each side of the main entrance, which I had often thought I would like to paint or sketch. While I was looking at these, a clergyman came up to me from the direction of the sundial, and spoke to me. He said: "You seem to be interested in the Cathedral," and I replied that I was, and had thought of trying to sketch the windows. The clergyman said that it was a very fine building and that there was a lot of beautiful work inside. After some minutes friendly conversation, the clergyman walked away. I attached no particular importance to the incident at the time, although when I saw the newspaper photographs of Archdeacon Wakeford I remembered the face as that of someone I had spoken to previously. I have now been shown several special photographs of Archdeacon Wakeford, and I identify him as the clergyman I talked with at the Cathedral.'

The girl confirmed that she had also passed the Cathedral later that morning, at about 11.30 a.m. when a sharp shower had driven her to seek cover inside. She decided that she would pass the time by looking at the picture of Old Scarlett. While she was doing this she met the clergyman again and after some polite conversation, she was taken by him to see the tombs of the two queens. It was still raining when she tried to leave the Cathedral, so she sheltered in the porch, and met the clergyman for a third time as he was leaving. He directed her to Caster's stationers shop where she bought a postcard of the picture of Old Scarlett. The old clergyman had walked off by himself in the rain.

'The Girl in the Cathedral' was a slim, nineteen-year-old woman, modest and quiet in manner, and with a clear, half-languid voice. Freda Hansen, wife of George Philip Hansen, was now living in Harborne, Birmingham. At Peterborough, Hansen had owned a bicycle shop where he also manufactured his own model, the Dinkum Cycle. However, the business was burnt to the ground after Hansen had

149

inadvertently filled a blowlamp with petrol; he was then in serious financial trouble. To escape his creditors, and the rumours which said that the fire had been started deliberately, Hansen fled to Birmingham, leaving his wife and baby daughter in Peterborough with his mother-in-law. Mrs Hansen later joined her husband at Harborne and was living there when she was run to ground by *John Bull*.

Freda Hansen vividly remembered her companion in Peterborough Cathedral. At the time she had thought he was a bishop, and had, in fact, spotted Wakeford on a second occasion when he came to the city in August trying to clear up the police evidence against him. Mrs Hansen mentioned it in an affectionate letter which she wrote to her husband ('My own Darling Billie') on 7th August: 'By the way, I do not know if ever I told you I saw my Cathedral friend some time ago. I passed him in the street, but I do not think he saw me. I was thinking of speaking to him, because as he is a Bishop he might be able to help us.'

Although she did not see him, Freda Hansen also had good reason to remember the weekend of Wakeford's second visit to Peterborough at Easter 1920. There were police everywhere, she noticed. Two of them even followed her and her husband to the theatre on the 3rd April and, afterwards, to their home. There, according to Freda Hansen, one of the policemen told her that she had to leave her husband and that George Hansen must get out of Peterborough forthwith, because of the debts which Hansen had run up in the city, owing to the loss of his bicycle business. Freda Hansen wondered: 'Did any of the police or anyone connected with the prosecution see me in the Cathedral on March 15th 1920?' Had they, in fact, tried to get her out of Peterborough to prevent her identifying, and thus exonerating, Archdeacon Wakeford?

★　　★　　★

John Wakeford met Freda Hansen in the *John Bull* offices in Long Acre on the 28th May 1921. He had no difficulty in recognising her as the girl in the Cathedral; there was the deprecatory movement of the lips and the way she turned her pear-shaped chin towards the left as she spoke. Freda Hansen got Wakeford to put on his coat and shovel hat to confirm her identification of him. Wakeford's feelings must have been very mixed, for this was the woman who — had she come forward at the trial — could have prevented his ruin, and who even now might prove his innocence. Charles Pilley, the tough journalist whom Horatio Bottomley had given special responsibility in the Wakeford case, was watching Wakeford closely. 'Never once did I detect so much as the quiver of an eyelid that might betray a hidden consciousness of guilt . . . If John Wakeford is a guilty man he is the most consummate actor of our time. If he is innocent his lion-hearted courage is beyond all praise.'

Mrs Hansen signed a statutory declaration that she had been with Archdeacon Wakeford in Peterborough Cathedral; her husband signed another declaring that he had seen his wife talking to Wakeford when he had gone to the Cathedral to meet her on the morning of 15th March 1920.

John Bull was cock-a-hoop at the discovery of the 'Girl in the Cathedral' and made great play with Birkenhead's pronouncement that 'a word from her would clear an innocent man'. No woman had come forward to testify that she had slept with the Archdeacon at the Bull Hotel, despite the newspaper's promises of anonymity: 'the conditions laid down by the Lord Chancellor as the single loophole of escape of this harassed cleric have been satisfied, and we feel no reason to be ashamed of the part we have played in relation to one of the most baffling mysteries of modern times'.

The 'Wakeford Drama' was staple entertainment for *John Bull* readers through the hot summer of 1921. Each issue brought fresh morsels, 'important announcements' and bellicose demands for justice.

151

On the 9th July, the cover promised fresh developments; inside, the readers were exhorted to come to Queen's Hall on 25th July at 8 p.m., when ex-Archdeacon Wakeford would address a 'mass meeting'. On the 16th July there were more sensations: a 'STARTLING WAKEFORD THEORY' (that the ex-Archdeacon *might* have had a 'double' who *could* have caused all the trouble at Peterborough), news that letters of support were pouring in and that there would be a cinematographic performance at the Queen's Hall meeting ('a great film — produced for the proprietors of *John Bull* by the Gaumont Company, Ltd., and embodying the main scenes in the Wakeford drama'). The following week there was a eulogy by the assistant editor — 'WHAT I THINK OF JOHN WAKEFORD' — who expressed his scepticism of the findings of the Judicial Committee of the Privy Council and called on 'every man and woman with a sense of fairplay, and a respect for the principles of British justice to ... hear from the ex-Archdeacon's own lips the great human story of which he is the central figure'.

Wakeford's performance at Queen's Hall was a tour de force. The building was jammed to the doors long before eight o'clock. It was the Thursday before the summer bank holiday, the weather was glorious and the assembly was in festive mood. John Wakeford held the audience in the palm of his hand; he had lost none of his oratorical powers and the listeners were spellbound as he went over the chain of events which had led to his humiliation and ruin. There were murmurs of sympathy and cries of 'the dirty dogs' at the mention of witnesses who had testified against Wakeford.

There was tumultuous applause at the end and then silence as the hall darkened for the film show. This was something quite out of the ordinary; a glimpse of real-life drama captured in moving pictures. The title, 'The Mystery of the Wakeford Case', flickered on to the screen: 'Produced for the *John Bull* newspaper by Mr Norman Ramsay, M.A.' The Archdeacon of Stow himself appeared next — full length and

152

in close-up — declaiming nobly in silence, his words shown in ornate sub-titles. Then the scene changed and the Archdeacon was shown telling his wife that he has to go on a journey. A maid is told to pack the bag. She slips only a nightshirt into a black handbag and the Archdeacon, thus equipped, takes leave of his wife and strides from the room.

The next scene is the interior of the Bull Hotel at Peterborough. Two men are quaffing mugs of beer in the lobby as the Archdeacon signs the register. He goes up to his room and is eventually shown wandering off to the Cathedral. Meanwhile, back in the hotel, the stealthy hand of an unseen writer is shown adding 'and wife' to the Archdeacon's signature in the book.

The silence which had preceded the show had become a subdued murmur. In the film, a young woman now appears, carefully examining the exterior of the cathedral porch with the Archdeacon. However, she seems to find it of little interest and tip taps jerkily away in the general direction of her husband, who is waiting for her in the distance. There were audible sniggers from the auditorium. Then Edmund and Mary Blunden appear briefly to re-enact the episode of the missing wedding ring.

The film approached its end with a glimpse of a pair of pyjamas and a nightdress lying side by side on a bed, followed by a sub-title: 'The pyjama theory falls through'. The final shot, which was greeted with open laughter, was of an immaculate bed with an old-fashioned nightshirt laid out on a single, virtuous pillow.

Charles Pilley, now the Assistant Editor of *John Bull*, had planned that the climax of the evening should be the passing of a mass resolution calling for the re-opening of the Wakeford Case. But the audience had had enough and what should have been a glorious start to John Wakeford's campaign for justice became a farce as the giggling crowd pushed from the stuffy hall into the cool air of a fine summer evening.

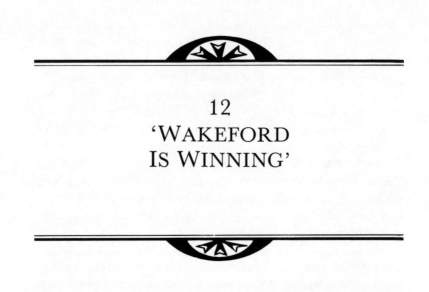

12
'WAKEFORD
IS WINNING'

Once the film had been made, 'ex-Archdeacon Wakeford' was obliged to run on the treadmill of public performances devised by Horatio Bottomley. He appeared all over England at 1s 3d or 2s 4d a seat (the best part of a labouring man's daily wage in 1921). On the 1st September at three o'clock in the afternoon he was in Colchester, that evening he appeared in Ipswich and remained there for two days; on the 4th he was at Southend-on-Sea, and then he moved on to Herne Bay, Canterbury, Margate, Deal, Folkestone, Redhill, Bournemouth, Stroud and Walthamstow, speaking in cinemas, town halls, theatres and ballrooms. The formula was always the same: first, Wakeford would speak, then Freda Hansen would appear briefly, amidst applause for her pluck in coming forward. Postcards of 'The Girl in the Cathedral' were sold in the interval; the finale was a showing of 'The Mystery of the Wakeford Case'.

By this time the film was also on general release and was shown in cinemas from Edinburgh to Bournemouth. And it was a success, for despite its disastrous London première it was well received in the provinces. The trade magazine, the

Bioscope, said that: 'This glimpse of a real-life drama — assuredly more strange than fiction — is singularly thrilling. Mr Wakeford's striking personality makes itself felt across the screen, and one feels that, although his appearance in such a picture is unprecedented, it is by no means undignified.' At the Kursaal Cinema at Southend the film earned the highest takings for any week in the year and the *Folkestone Express* reported large audiences at the Electric Cinema. The critic of the *East Anglian Times* was convinced by the showing at the Vaudeville, Colchester, 'especially by that part showing the alleged writing of the Archdeacon in the visitor's book at the Bull Hotel, Peterborough, in which it was plain to see that the words "and wife" were inserted in quite another writing'.

At the beginning of October 1921, Wakeford and Freda Hansen, chaperoned by her mother, were launched on an extended lecture tour of the Midlands. They started in the south, at Watford, and then as the days shortened moved to Northampton, Leamington Spa, Coventry, Birmingham, West Bromwich, Wednesbury, Walsall, Aston, Sutton Cold-field and Wolverhampton, Hanley and Stoke-on-Trent. Everywhere, meeting halls were packed to the doors; everywhere, resolutions were enthusiastically passed, expressing belief in Wakeford's innocence; money poured into the *John Bull* coffers.

Charles Pilley was now in virtual control of *John Bull* and of Wakeford's campaign, for Horatio Bottomley was in difficulties: his former business partner, Reuben Bigland, outraged by Bottomley's refusal to join him in a fraudulent scheme to produce petrol from water, sacrificed himself by parading in a black mask outside the *John Bull* offices and Bottomley's other haunts, selling copies of a pamphlet entitled: 'The Downfall of Horatio Bottomley, M.P. His Latest and Greatest Swindle'. Infuriated by Bigland's street hawkers crying outside the Eccentric Club in St James's, Bottomley finally lost his temper and brought legal action against his tormentor. Bigland gave himself up to the

THE PUBLIC HALL

THURSDAY, September 1st *at* 8 *o'clock*

DOORS OPEN at 7.30.

Ex-ARCHDEACON WAKEFORD,

ONE OF THE FINEST ORATORS
of the day,

will give his GREAT ADDRESS on

'The Wakeford Mystery."

Messrs. GAUMONT'S Topical Film of the
event will be shown, and

" The Girl in the Cathedral"

will be present.

Two prices only:—

2s. 4d. and 1s. 3d., including tax.

Seats can be booked at the Hall.

Newspaper advertisement for 'The Wakeford Mystery'

Birmingham police on the 3rd October and set in motion the trial that was to ruin Bottomley by the exposure of his swindling financial practices. Bottomley gave up the editorship of *John Bull* to Charles Pilley in December 1921.

It was Pilley, following Bottomley's idea, who advised Wakeford to make a fresh approach to the Judicial Committee of the Privy Council. A letter was drafted, and duly published in *John Bull*, in which Wakeford pointed out that he had been at a 'considerable disadvantage through the

156

absence of an essential witness', who had now been discovered, and asked for direction as to what further procedures he should adopt 'to satisfy the requirements of justice'.

The reply came from the Clerk to the Privy Council, in a bleak note dated the 10th October, 1921.

Sir,

Referring to your letter of the 22nd September, I am directed to say in reply that it is open to you to consult your legal advisers — if you think it desirable — on the point raised.

I am, Sir,
Your obedient servant,
Almeric FitzRoy

There was no more talk of a direct approach to the Privy Council. Only one course remained: an appeal to the King. For this, all the ballyhoo of *John Bull* was mobilised. Charles Pilley knocked out a book, *The Secret History of the Wakeford Case*: a 'striking volume', according to *John Bull*, containing 'much startling information hitherto not made available to the general public'. It cost a shilling and was, in fact, largely a re-hash of the articles with which Pilley's readers had been surfeited for the preceding weeks. But such was public interest in the tragedy of John Wakeford it sold like hot cakes. Then on the 10th December there were headlines announcing 'WAKEFORD'S DRAMATIC APPEAL', and calling for a million signatures for a 'monster petition to the King', a cause 'which every British citizen, from the highest to the lowest should be proud to lend a hand'. Each week were listed the people and places from which petition forms could be obtained, from vicarages and *John Bull* pen shops, business addresses and private homes from Ashton-in-Makerfield to Cologne.

John Bull readers were promised 'amazing revelations', 'important developments' and 'fresh evidence of conspiracy'. The news was given that Evelyn Wakeford had received a letter concerning: 'an individual who has borne a not inconspicuous part in the chain of events leading up to the present day'. It was printed in full, omitting only the name of the 'individual' and the signature; with a request from Mrs Wakeford for the writer to come forward.

> Dear Mrs Wakeford,
>
> I am very sorry indeed to hear of the grief —— has brought upon you and the Canon. I cannot give any particulars of the movements of the Canon on the dates mentioned, but I can say this. I was away three times last year, staying at different hotels with ——, and he said he was planning to destroy the Canon's reputation. When I told him what a dirty dog he was, he said he was only getting his own back. We had a quarrel and I have not seen him since November.
>
> Yours respectfully,
> ————

—— is a decent chum while he can have all he wants, but once rubbed the wrong way he is a perfect devil. I was once frightened of him, but I am not now. I am surprised at the evidence being taken from such a man. I thought he was a widower intending to marry me.

In a generous two-page spread, with a cartoon showing a be-wigged and gowned John Bull knocking at the door of the 'Hall of Justice', the letter-writer was asked to contact Mrs Wakeford, for no address had been given — only a Nottingham postmark on the envelope. Followers of the Wakeford Case speculated about — and took bets on — the identity of the 'dirty dog'. Was he C.T. Moore (who had certainly wanted to 'get his own back', but he was, after all, seventy-three years old and had *not* given evidence on the case) or conceivably Worthington or perhaps Tuplin (who was a friend of 'Mrs Ellis' and might have sought revenge), or was it all just a hoax?

There was no response to Evelyn Wakeford's request. Two

weeks later, *John Bull* carried the following cryptic message. 'I shall be glad if Maud Pace will write to me again. Evelyn M. Wakeford.'

Maud Pace did not respond, nor was she found. But the spicy intervention further coloured the Wakeford Case with the suggestion of sinister conspiracy and was thoroughly exploited in the pages of *John Bull*.

Support for John Wakeford was not confined to Bottomley's journal, however. The *Sunday Express* ran the 'full story' of the 'Girl in the Cathedral'; Edmund Blunden was still plugging away in the pages of *The Nation and the Athenaeum* 'I think that the public will soon have to make up their minds that they have not heard the last of the Wakeford Case and that the growing desire for a rehearing cannot be denied much longer.' Hugh Massingham wrote in identical vein in the *Westminster Gazette*.

Then an unexpected ally materialised. Margaret Tyler was a middle-aged spinster with a wig; she was the author of several text books, and the most distinguished homeopathic physician of her time. She had a passionate regard for justice and with characteristic energy she compiled a detailed critique of the Wakeford Case, based largely on the evidence presented to the Privy Council Committee. The results were set out in a penny booklet, published at the expense of the author (M.L.T.), listing on each page the conflicting evidence in two parallel columns: the pros on the left, the cons on the right.

For Margaret Tyler, there was only one possible con-clusion: Wakeford was innocent; there was only one 'sane solution' to the mystery: that he had been impersonated. According to the doctor, two men and a woman would be required to achieve this. The deed would have been carried out sometime during the Archdeacon's visits to Peter-borough; inquiries would have been made later, to allow memories to become blunted. These would have been accompanied by the judicious distribution of half-crowns, and all that was then necessary was to set tongues wagging, and wits to work, striving to recall the impersonator's visits to the Bull Hotel.

According to Dr Tyler's theory, one of the villains involved must have resembled the Archdeacon and carried a small suitcase containing theatrical properties. Most probably he would have used a facial disguise (blue glasses and a moustache and beard) when not actually engaged in the impersonation and would certainly have made a close study of the Archdeacon's dress, demeanour and walk. The second man kept watch and acted as go-between. When the Archdeacon was safely out of the way (in the Cathedral or walking in the countryside or on the train for Lincoln) then the look out would give the go-ahead for the impersonator to parade the woman around the tapestry school, appear with her at the Bull Hotel, visit the church at Stanground and, as a last bold flourish, to walk with her at Peterborough Station when the real Archdeacon was on his way back to Lincoln.

This, Dr Tyler was convinced, was the means by which Archdeacon Wakeford was brought down. But, for her, there was more to it than that: 'What was the Unseen Hand that so successfully pulled the strings? With whom was Moore in touch? How many were in the conspiracy, and how many more were dupes?' Worse: 'Was there the Big Thing behind this, that looms so darkly behind other of these persecutions of the Clergy of the Church of England? For Archdeacon Wakeford's case is, after all, only one of many; and in their main features and plan of campaign, they are strikingly alike'.

So, for the most distinguished homeopathic physician of her generation, the Wakeford Case was part of a national conspiracy for the destruction of high-churchmen. It was a theme skilfully embroidered in the pages of *John Bull*: a singular irony for a journal in which for years erring clergymen had been prime targets.

★   ★   ★

21 Edward Carson and
F.E. Smith inspecting
Ulster volunteers at
Dromore, Co. Down, 1913

22 Lord Chancellor
Birkenhead, 1920

23 *Left* Douglas Hogg, 1924   24 *Right* Edmund Blunden, ca 1925

25 Photographs of Wakeford's entries in the visitors' book at the
Bull Hotel, Peterborough, published in *John Bull*

THE VITAL SIGNATURES.

March 14th, 1920.

April 2nd, 1920.

26 Horatio Bottomley arriving at Bow Street for the police prosecution of Reuben Bigland, October 1921; on his right is his accountant, Arthur Newton, on the left his manservant, George Rawson

27 John Wakeford after the appeal court verdict, April 1921

28 Freda Hansen with her husband, ca 1920

As the spring of 1922 approached, Wakeford was still on the road lecturing in echoing drill halls, ornate new cinemas and draughty hired rooms. But his appearances were losing their impact and 'The Girl in the Cathedral' had been unable to stand the pace, having nearly died of influenza in Newcastle.

John Bull continued to announce the ex-Archdeacon's willingness to appear at any place, with or without a lantern slide show or film performance. There were euphoric reports on the progress of the appeal to the King. Each week, fresh lists of the names and addresses of sympathisers from whom petition forms could be obtained were printed beneath stirring headlines: 'ALL FOR WAKEFORD', 'RALLY ROUND WAKEFORD', 'WAKEFORD IS WINNING'.

On the 4th April 1922, John Wakeford carried his petition to the Home Office. He needed help from a group of clergymen who went with him, for the thousands of petition forms had been stuck together to form a gigantic roll weighing more than half a hundredweight. It was a clear sunny morning and King Charles Street was packed with waiting onlookers and newspaper reporters, pushing and jostling for a glimpse and a few more defiant phrases from the ex-Archdeacon of Stow.

It was stale news by the following Saturday, when the next issue of *John Bull* appeared. The paper was thoroughly piqued that 'none of our graceful contemporaries has seen fit to mention the fact that the petition handed in last Tuesday in the presence of a battery of press photographers and reporters was organised and carried through *entirely* by *John Bull*.' Under the headline 'WHY WAKEFORD WILL WIN' Charles Pilley struggled to keep up the pressure with a final message from Wakeford: 'I have never asked for pity; I do not ask for favour; I ask only for justice.' 'It is our conviction,' Pilley concluded, 'that this stern and uphill fight is nearly won.'

And there *John Bull* was wrong: the petition failed. The confident prediction of victory was the last word on the Wakeford Case that appeared in Horatio Bottomley's rag.

Oft at the portal of the Hall
Has John Bull knocked in vain

But Justice yet shall heed the call
And ope the door again!

Defeated, ex-Archdeacon Wakeford was a liability and they dropped him like a hot cake. The chances of success had in reality been infinitesimal, for although it would have been theoretically possible for the Sovereign to have referred the case back to the Judicial Committee of the Privy Council there seem to have been no instances where this has actually happened. Bottomley and his successor, Pilley, a barrister-at-law, must have known this. But Wakeford had served his turn — and so had the 'Girl in the Cathedral' who never received her £2000 reward. They had sold copies of *John Bull* and filled cinemas all over the country for months on end. Now the country was tired of them.

13
AFTERMATH

After their expulsion from the Cathedral Close at Lincoln the Wakefords moved to a small, brick and plaster bungalow, which they called Polesteeple House, in a muddy Kentish lane. They had been invited to Biggin Hill by a clergyman who had known and admired John Wakeford in his Liverpool days. Brian O'Laughlin had been Vicar of Cudham since leaving the army in 1918; Biggin Hill was part of his parish. It was a raw, end-of-the-line sort of place, a mushrooming township of scattered bungalows and rickety weekend chalets, but property was cheap and people could live anonymous lives there without much interference.

The lane was overgrown and enclosed, like a steep leafy tunnel, with the Wakefords' bungalow at the end. From the wooden verandah of the house there was a depressing view of a scrubby hillside and make-shift houses. Opposite was a tin hut used as a mission hall and nearby stood a corrugated iron church, with a paraffin-smelling, varnished matchboard interior, thrown up to cater for the raw young parish.

John Wakeford had told the newspapermen in Downing Street that he had been asked by the incumbent to provide pastoral care for a place in the diocese of Rochester and it was at Biggin Hill that he came to rest. There was little for him to do in the aftermath of his defeat: there was already a curate at Biggin Hill and the local people were wary of the notorious ex-Archdeacon Wakeford. He was a priest without a ministry and this was his greatest torment; he could no longer raise his great voice in public worship of the risen Christ.

Wakeford became a familiar figure in the lanes and byways of Biggin Hill. He still wore clerical black. He was always walking alone, always purposefully, leaning slightly forward as though hurrying on an urgent errand; his long face was haggard and deeply lined. His whole existence was dominated by the need to prove his innocence, but he spoke little of his sense of outrage. It was Evelyn Wakeford who protested her husband's innocence to the customers in Temple's grocery shop and more privately to the friends she made in Biggin Hill.

In 1923 there came, by pure chance, a last painful opportunity to clear his name. It came to the ears of Wakeford's supporter Dr Margaret Tyler that Henry Wright had been boasting of the part he had played in the Wakeford case. He was unwilling to relinquish this important role and spent a good deal of time explaining to anyone who would listen his vital part in securing the failure of the appeal. He had now embellished the story, claiming that he had frequently followed the Archdeacon to hotels with women: Wakeford, he said, with the cheap charity of the righteous man, 'would be a very nice fellow if he would only keep the Seventh Commandment'. But he boasted once too often − in this case to his Vicar, the Reverend George Neatby of St John's Church, Highgate — and the news got back to Dr Tyler, because Neatby's brother was a physician at the same hospital.

Wakeford brought an action of slander against Wright. It was heard in the King's Bench Division in October 1923. Margaret Tyler took a prominent part in the proceedings; she saw a glimmer of hope in airing the silly 'impersonation theory' which she had formulated in her penny pamphlet. But the action failed, largely on a legal nicety (based on the case of Gallwey v. Marshall, 1853) that 'an action by a person in Holy Orders was not sustainable for words spoken of him as a clergyman unless he was holding office': Wakeford was, of course, not holding office when Henry Wright was entertaining his acquaintances with colourful accounts of the Archdeacon's private life. Wakeford had to pay Wright's costs of £597.

This was the final blow. Wakeford had now incurred debts of over five thousand pounds and faced financial ruin. In 1924 he was declared bankrupt and brought to court by Henry Wright for the recovery of legal costs. Help came from an appeal fund which was launched by four bishops. Wakeford was discharged from bankruptcy in April 1924 and, with his wife's income from poultry keeping, they were able to eke out an existence in the bungalow on Polesteeple Hill.

Wakeford became just another Biggin Hill character, to be dimly remembered years later, with knowing winks, along with other local eccentrics like Rolla Richards, who peddled round on a tricycle with a black cat perched on his shoulder, or Dummy Hankins, the amiable deaf mute who made funny guttural sounds. Some villagers were touched by the intensity and occasional sweetness of the sombre man with the clear blue eyes who meekly accompanied Mrs Wakeford to the meetings of the Biggin Hill Horticultural and Fanciers Association or the Cudham and District Nursing Association. But few in Biggin Hill cared one way or the other whether the Archdeacon of Stow had taken a girl to the Bull Hotel in Peterborough: it was 'nothing to the world whether one man goes up or down'.

It was a great day for Wakeford when a letter came to Polesteeple Hill from Liverpool or from Sub-Dean Leeke, who found time regularly to write to John Wakeford from

Lincoln. Leeke's last letter came in March 1925 not long before he died: 'I have never doubted but that these stories, to which you allude and the truth of which you set yourself to disprove, are mere figments'.

★   ★   ★

One Sunday afternoon, some months later, John Perkins, the churchwarden, opened the door of his house in Anfield to find John Wakeford knocking for admittance. Tired, dusty and penniless, Wakeford had walked more than two hundred miles north to Liverpool. He then called on Leonard Rich, his successor at Anfield, and asked if he could speak to the children at the Sunday School. Rich, a kindly man, led the strange dishevelled figure in and John Wakeford spoke again to the rows of scrubbed, clean children, sitting on the wooden forms in the gloomy schoolroom, as he had done so many times before. The news quickly spread that Wakeford had returned to Anfield. A girl of eighteen called Margaret Foxcroft came late — just as the children were coming out — for she had been teaching an overflow class in the old Lombard Street building in West Derby Road. She knew Wakeford well from the large photograph of him which hung in her aunt's sitting room, and was shocked by his appearance and by how much he had aged. Her sister Alice had heard him talk and, like the others who were crowding round him, her eyes were still shining with the excitement of what he had said. It was Wakeford's last triumph as an orator.

That evening he was 'tidied up' — as he had been as a boy by the old Rabbi in Devonport who had led him to religion — and John Perkins collected money to get him home. They bought him a ticket and put him on the train back to Kent.

★   ★   ★

The lonely years he spent at Biggin Hill put an intolerable

pressure on his sanity. Wakeford's mind began to crumble and in March 1928 he was locked away. Like Lear, the wonder was that he had 'endur'd so long'.

Early on a February morning in 1930, John Wakeford had a heart attack and became unconscious. His wife went to his bedside at the Barming Heath asylum and remained with him until just before noon, when his condition seemed to have improved. Wakeford died a few minutes after she had returned to Biggin Hill to feed the hens.

They buried him in Cudham churchyard. His oak coffin was inscribed: 'John Wakeford, Priest'.

PART FOUR

EPILOGUE

14
WAS WAKEFORD GUILTY?

So many strands of John Wakeford's turbulent life came together when he walked into the lobby of the Bull Hotel in March 1920. His ability to antagonise his fellow clergymen was fully developed even when, as a young man, he dreamed of dedicating his life to poverty and celibacy, only to incur the enmity of Charles Atherton and Bishop Bickersteth. The seed of hatred within his own family was sown in 1893, when he returned to Northlew to marry Herbert Worthington's sister against her brother's wishes. The years in Liverpool linked him unjustly with the legend of the high-church womaniser, despoiler of postmen's wives, and the calumny stuck to him at Lincoln. It provided ammunition for Dean Fry. And when C.T. Moore swore he would be revenged on Wakeford for bringing him to trial and depriving him of the living at Kirkstead, the absurd legend grew up around Wakeford like a parasite and choked him. The bizarre chance, that of all the parishes in England his brother-in-law's should adjoin Moore's at Appleby Magna, enabled Wakeford's most implacable enemy to draw the trap tight.

★   ★   ★

The Privy Council's belief in Wakeford's guilt rested largely on four lines of reasoning.

First, there was the girl in the Cathedral. Far from requiring proof of her identity, Birkenhead in his judgment held that her very absence signalled guilt: 'surely an innocent woman would not have been so callous as to obstinately hold her peace when a word from her would have cleared Wakeford?'

Then there was the matter of the hotel books. This had been Birkenhead's particular enthusiasm, peering through a magnifying glass at the entries in the register, noticing the similarities of the 'and wife' to Wakeford's writing with its characteristic dotting of the 'i's. For Birkenhead 'the writing in such circumstances furnishes overwhelming corroboration of the evidence'.

The third line of reasoning concerned the so-called 'independent witnesses', notably the hide and wool buyer from Worcester, Harold Osborne and his wife and, to a lesser extent, the Vicar of Stanground and the ladies from the tapestry school, who all claimed to have seen Wakeford in the company of an unidentified female companion during his first visit to Peterborough in March 1920. According to Birkenhead, the law lords and the clerical assessors had been most strongly swayed by Osborne's evidence that he had seen Wakeford with a young woman on the night of the 14th March and again at breakfast on the following morning in the private room at the Bull. Their lordships had been particularly impressed by the fact that the Osbornes' testimonies had been offered spontaneously and that Mr Osborne appeared to be 'a man of considerable intelligence'.

Finally, there was Birkenhead's clinching argument against a conspiracy, namely the improbability that a trap could have been set in advance by Moore and Worthington. After all, Wakeford chose the Bull Hotel without telling anyone where he would stay: 'By what amazing coincidence did it come about that the Appellant should have selected on this occasion the one hotel in Peterborough whose landlord was ready to be corrupted, able to carry with him into this maze of slander and perjury his wife and his servants, and zealous to commence a systematic course of forgery in support of the plan?'

The discovery of Freda Hansen removed the first plank of the Privy Council judgment. Her testimony and that of her husband, both sworn before an attorney, were as admissible as if they had been delivered before the Judicial Committee of the Privy Council where Birkenhead had said that her appearance 'would clear an innocent man'.

Freda Hansen's statement, together with those of the Dean of Peterborough and the Verger, also confirmed that Archdeacon Wakeford had been in the Cathedral, as he swore, from about 10.15 a.m. to 12.30 p.m. on the 15th March, evidence which flatly contradicted that of the two seamstresses who claimed that the Archdeacon had lingered for an hour in the tapestry school with a young woman from about 11.00 or 11.30 that same morning. Their evidence was, in fact, doubly suspect for they said that Wakeford had visited the school during a heavy snowstorm: the official meteorological report, for Peterborough, records only 'rain and sleet' on the day in question.

Birkenhead's second plank, the entries in the hotel register, is one of the most surprising aspects of the Wakeford Case. The prosecution witness, the hand-writing expert Charles Mitchell, stated quite unequivocally that he was unable to decide as to the authenticity of the writings in the register. Why then should Birkenhead, with the knowledge that Pugh had admitted doctoring Wakeford's entries, take it upon himself to give a clear ruling on these matters even to the extent of declaring that they furnished 'overwhelming corroboration' of the other evidence of Wakeford's guilt?

Despite his enthusiasm for graphology, Birkenhead

173

failed to spot a vital clue in Wakeford's entry in the hotel register for his second stay at the Bull on the 2nd April 1920:

J. Wakeford and wife 8 Precincts, Lincoln

M. Wakeford M.   8   ,,   ,,

Now, Wakeford testified that he wrote only his name and address in the register. These were clearly written. However, all the remaining writings ('and wife', the two '8s' and 'M. Wakeford M') were slightly, but definitely, *smeared*, as though smudged by a single awkward movement of the blotting paper. So Wakeford's signature and his address must have been *dry* and the rest of the writing *wet* when it was blotted, even though 'and wife' came between the signature and the address. Even more suspicious was the fact that the '8s' in the centre column of the page had been written over two figure '5s'. What is more, the '5s' were clear and the '8s' smudged.

Clearly, someone had tampered with the hotel book. There are two possibilities: the alterations were made by Wakeford (when Mrs Pugh, as she claimed, had taken the register to his bedroom) *or* someone else in the hotel doctored the entry.

The first possibility fitted with Douglas Hogg's contention, made in his opening remarks to the appeal court, that Mrs Pugh had brought the book to Wakeford's room on his second visit to the hotel in April. Yet in her evidence Mrs Pugh said that she took the register to Wakeford on his *first* visit, on the 15th March.

Furthermore, according to the police witnesses, both Wakeford *and* his alleged female companion signed the register in the lobby on the Archdeacon's second visit to the hotel. In this case, it would have been unnecessary for the register to have been taken up for the addition of the supposed woman's signature (the smudged 'M. Wakeford M').

The evidence of the hotel register, far from supporting Birkenhead's contention, suggests the very reverse, namely, that the second entry must have been doctored and by someone other than Wakeford: a view that was also held by a handwriting expert from the British Museum who later examined the book ('the questioned part of the entry in the visitors' book is, in my opinion, a fraudulent addition with some attempt at simulation of the Archdeacon's hand-writing').

The law lords' uncritical acceptance of the Osbornes' testimony is another astonishing aspect of the appeal court hearing. Harold Osborne claimed that he had seen Arch-deacon Wakeford and the woman taking breakfast together in the small private room on the morning of the 15th March. According to Osborne, Archdeacon Wakeford and the woman were sitting at the table near the french windows *together with Mr and Mrs Pugh*. Yet the Pughs made no mention of this in their evidence. It is inconceivable that they could have spent some time sitting in close proximity to Wakeford and his alleged companion without mentioning this totally damning fact at some stage in their testimonies, or during prolonged cross-examinations. Furthermore, it is very difficult to believe that a hotel manager and his wife would in any case have eaten breakfast at the same table as their guests, especially when one of them was a senior church dignitary. In the face of the evidence of several other guests that Arch-deacon Wakeford breakfasted by himself in the dining-room on the morning of the 15th March 1920, the Osbornes' recollection looks even more improbable.

There was also conflict between the Osbornes' evidence and that of other witnesses. For example, Mr Osborne swore that the grill room was not used during the weekend and that the tables and chairs were all piled up on top of each other. Hence, according to this, Wakeford could only have taken breakfast in the private room on the morning of the 15th March and eaten there on the previous evening, Sunday. Yet Seymour Hicks's entire theatrical company had dined in the grill room that night; indeed there was nowhere else they could have done so for they were not in the public dining-room and could not have been accommodated in the small private room.

So, as Edmund Blunden suspected at the time, Osborne's testimony was flawed and far from proving Wakeford's guilt, as Birkenhead maintained, it suggested quite the reverse: that the wool and hide buyer and his wife, who incredibly was in court while he gave his evidence, had lied or were badly mistaken.

The remaining buttress of Birkenhead's judgment was the sheer improbability that a trap could have been set for Wakeford on his first visit to Peterborough, for no one knew in advance that he would stay at the Bull Hotel. This is at first sight a convincing argument against conspiracy, but it ignores a very obvious possibility: that conspiracy occurred not before, but *after* the event.

There was plenty of time — as much as four months — before Worthington finally revealed to his sister the possibility that her husband would be brought to trial, and by that time C.T. Moore's private eye, Agar, had already visited the Bull Hotel and did so on three separate occasions. Furthermore, it *was* known that Wakeford intended to stay at the Bull on his second visit, because he sent a postcard to Pugh reserving a room for the night of the 2nd April 1920.

As Birkenhead revealed, the law lords were deeply suspicious of the part played by the hotel staff and the Peterborough police in the Wakeford Case. They had good reason to be, for the Pughs and their friend Tuplin, the chambermaid and the waitresses, like the police involved, either lied or made garbled, contradictory statements.

Pugh, in particular, showed himself to be an incompetent liar. He repeatedly denied adding the words 'and wife' to Wakeford's first entry in the hotel register before admitting, under Edward Carson's bludgeoning, that he had in fact done so. Pugh also claimed that he did not recognise Wakeford on his first visit to the Bull and was forced to send his wife to examine the Archdeacon's night clothes in order to read the name tape. Yet Tuplin swore that Pugh had told him that he recognised Wakeford from the outset ('Don't you know who that is?'). Then there was Pugh's sworn identification of Evelyn Porter as the woman with Wakeford in the hotel: a claim which he later retracted under cross-examination.

The hotel servants were equally unreliable. One waitress said that Wakeford dined in the grill room, the other that he was in the private room on the 14th March. Both women remembered Wakeford as breakfasting in the private room, while Pugh claimed that the Archdeacon ate in the grill room on the following morning. The attribution to Wakeford of Edmund Blunden's jocular remark ('Mary, take your hands off the table or they will throw you out of the place') is a notable example of garbled recollections extracted — weeks after the event — from busy, harassed women.

Birkenhead also had the measure of the police witnesses: their evidence was 'in part untrue and in part misleading', delivered with a 'lack of candour' and 'even positive mis-statements'.

The police account of the affair was as follows. Police-Sergeant King said that he saw Archdeacon Wakeford enter the Bull Hotel with a lady between twenty-five and thirty years of age; the Archdeacon went into the hotel office and signed the visitors' book while the woman waited in the corridor. Sergeant King was quite certain that the time was between 6.00 and 6.30 p.m. on the *15th March*: the day *after* Pugh swore that Wakeford signed the register. King later inspected the book, could not decipher Wakeford's signature, but testified that the address ('Precincts, Lincoln') was there.

Sergeant King at first maintained that the Peterborough police were on the look-out for a clergyman who was passing false cheques (although King later admitted under cross-examination that the clergyman had been gaoled in 1917) and, according to his account, dispatched P.C. Hall to keep an eye on the 'suspicious people at the Bull Hotel'. Later that evening, P.C. Hall appeared at the Bull and inspected

177

Wakeford's entry in the register. According to his evidence, he found a name but, unlike his superior, *no address*.

P.C. Hall's account differs in several other respects from that of the Sergeant. According to his testimony, he and another police constable were approached *in the street* by Archdeacon Wakeford, who had a woman with him, and were asked where they could get a bath. The policemen then followed them to the Grand Hotel. Hall claimed that he returned to the Bull, leaving the other constable on watch outside the Grand Hotel, and checked Wakeford's entry in the hotel register.

P.C. Hall testified that he later visited Canon Morse of Peterborough Cathedral to 'enquire' about Archdeacon Wakeford. A fourth policeman (a P.C. Smith) also seems to have been involved in the same errand. He said that he too visited Canon Morse (who was 'busy' and refused to see him) and then went to the Dean of Peterborough 'to inquire about a bishop and a lady staying at the Bull'. The Dean 'looked up the name in a Clerical Dictionary' and told the policeman that he had seen Wakeford in the Cathedral with a lady. According to P.C. Smith, he also saw the woman and the Archdeacon enter the Bull Hotel after 8.30 p.m. on the evening of the 15th March.

The police were also deeply involved in Archdeacon Wakeford's second visit to Peterborough. Sergeant King was, according to his testimony, actually waiting in the Bull Hotel, with Tuplin and Pugh, on the evening of Good Friday 1920, and saw Wakeford *and* the lady sign the register. Now, unless it was pure coincidence, King had no valid reason whatever for being at the Bull Hotel that night, for the Peterborough police had already established that Wakeford was not the clergyman who had been passing false cheques three years previously. Furthermore, King's testimony — that he saw both the Archdeacon and the woman sign the register — is impossible to reconcile with the curious smudging of Wakeford's entry which could only have been made if it had been carried out on two separate occasions.

The police part in the Wakeford Case was made even more dubious by Freda Hansen's statement that two policemen had later told her and her husband to clear out of Peterborough. What is more, they offered them a pound for their expenses. The implication was that with the girl in the Cathedral out of Peterborough, it would have been more difficult for her to have come forward to produce the evidence which, as Birkenhead said, 'would have cleared an innocent man'.

The lies and conflicting evidence by the hotel staff, Tuplin, Osborne and the Peterborough police are exactly what would be expected in a conspiracy to bring Wakeford down. As Birkenhead saw, such a scheme could not have been con- cocted before Wakeford's first visit or, possibly, even before his second stay at the Bull Hotel.

That a distinguished-looking ecclesiastic ('dressed like a bishop') should have stayed at a seedy commercial hotel was, itself, a matter of note in the socially sensitive society of a small cathedral town in the early 1920s. Add to this the fact that Archdeacon Wakeford was seen by the Dean and the Verger in the company of a young woman in Peterborough Cathedral, and was spotted afterwards by P.C. Smith among others when he directed her to Caster's card shop, you have the perfect scenario for small town gossips already fed on a diet of 'dirty old clergymen' by the popular press, notably by Horatio Bottomley's paper — which ironically became the Archdeacon's defender.

Whatever their reasons — whether from police station folklore about the fraudulent clergyman of 1917 or merely routine curiosity about anything unusual going on in their patch — the Peterborough police were sniffing round at the Bull Hotel within hours of Wakeford's arrival. Despite Pugh's disclaimer, it seems likely that the identity of his strange guest was known from the outset. Most extraordinary of all was the presence of Pugh's acquaintance, Frank Tuplin, at the Bull when Wakeford walked into the hotel on the evening of the 14th March 1920. This was an unlucky coincidence, as far as Wakeford was concerned, for Tuplin was a Lincoln man who knew Wakeford by sight. What is more, Tuplin was a friend of Daisy Ratcliffe, the self-styled 'Mrs Ellis' who had lived with C.T. Moore's caretaker at Kirkstead, and later kept the 'house of ill-repute' in Lincoln, the staying at which had brought Moore to trial, as he believed, at Archdeacon Wakeford's instigation.

So it is conceivable, despite Birkenhead's opinion, that C.T. Moore could have known in advance of Wakeford's intention to stay at the hotel on his second visit to Peterborough. This would account for the fact that Sergeant King and Frank Tuplin were both waiting with Pugh in the lobby when Wakeford walked into the Bull Hotel on the evening of Good Friday 1920: the only alternative explanations being sheer coincidence or pure mischief on the part of a police officer and the manager of the drapery department of the Peterborough Cooperative stores.

However, according to Herbert Worthington's curiously evasive version of events, he first learned of the gossip surrounding Wakeford's visits to Peterborough at dinner with his Bishop during a ruridecanal meeting on the 31st May 1920. Worthington further maintained that he did not speak to his neighbour and sporting companion until the 14th June when he visited the Rectory at Appleby Magna to commiserate with Mrs Moore under the mistaken impression that her husband had been killed in a riding accident. Having discovered that his friend's injuries were not fatal, Worthington said that he took up the matter of Wakeford's visits to Peterborough with the recovered C.T. Moore, in early July, immediately before the meeting with Mrs Wakeford at Burton-on-Trent railway station.

Worthington's confirmation that his sister had not accompanied her husband to the Bull Hotel left the way free for Moore to close the trap on Wakeford. The fact that Moore's cook had married a policeman — Agar — who was

180

willing to turn detective, was yet another unfortunate coincidence for Archdeacon Wakeford. Surprisingly, no one at the Consistory Court or the Privy Council Appeal sought to discover the identity of the mysterious bumpkin who ferreted about so assiduously after Wakeford's trail at Peterborough and received only £2 18s for his expenses. He was, in fact, the Superintendent of Police for Loughborough. Fred Agar had certainly started his career as a young bobby at Appleby Magna, where he had also courted the Moore children's governess before marrying the cook. Good humoured and seventeen stone, Agar was much attached to the Rector of Appleby Magna. Furthermore, like Charles Moore, he was a Freemason — one who had sworn on his bended knee to assist a brother Mason in adversity on pain of being 'severed in two' and his 'bowels burned to ashes' — and thus able to expect help from masonic colleagues in the Peterborough force.

Fred Agar visited Peterborough on three separate occasions in the late summer of 1920. Each time he talked to Mr and Mrs Pugh, to the staff of the Bull Hotel, to Frank Tuplin and to the assortment of witnesses who claimed to have seen Archdeacon Wakeford in the Cathedral or in the streets of Peterborough. From witness after witness Agar patiently extracted confused and conflicting statements: these ranged from the inadequate attempts of Alice Blisset, Mrs Willcocks and the other hotel servants to reconstruct — months later — dimly-remembered events from the turmoil of the Bull Hotel on Horse Fair night to downright lies by Pugh about his tinkering with the hotel register. Yet to the good-natured Police Superintendent, bent on helping a brother Mason of high degree, it must have seemed simply a matter of tidying up the facts to prove what was so patently obvious.

Herbert Worthington, who was evasive almost to the point of dishonesty about Agar's activities at Peterborough, carried the results of the Superintendent's hard work to the Bishop of Peterborough, and then to Bishop Swayne at Lincoln.

Wakeford's decision to clear his name by voluntarily submitting himself for trial at the Consistory Court played directly into the hands of his principal enemy at Lincoln, for Dean Fry could now take a hand in the proceedings. It was Fry who employed another investigator, Henry Wright, the managing clerk of the Bishop's solicitors, to retrace Agar's steps and produce what Edmund Blunden called 'this bundle of frail or rotten sticks': the ramshackle evidence that damned Archdeacon Wakeford before the Judicial Committee of the Privy Council.

Henry Wright seems to have been infected with Fry's malice towards Wakeford. He even boasted — and then later denied having said it — that he had *himself* traced the Archdeacon to hotels with women. It was Wright who dug out the final group of witnesses against Wakeford: all of whom swore that they had seen Wakeford with a young woman on his first visit to Peterborough, and their evidence was contradictory and inadequate.

Yet none of these later witnesses who were paraded before Birkenhead and his peers made as much impact as Harold Osborne and his wife. Their evidence, volunteered at the eleventh hour, more than that of any of the other witnesses swayed the case against Wakeford. It was the apparent impartiality and the fact that their evidence 'was offered spontaneously' that so impressed the Lord Chancellor and eliminated any possibility of their involvement in a conspiracy against Wakeford. Yet, as was not revealed in court, but was later discovered by Edmund Blunden, the Osbornes were close friends of the Pughs. This, no doubt, accounted for the fact that the Osbornes' names did not appear in the hotel register. Furthermore, as Edmund Blunden also discovered, there *was* another woman, besides his wife, staying in the Bull Hotel at the time of the Horse Fair. According to Blunden, the hotel accounts were kept by a young woman. She, however, was ill at the time of Wakeford's first visit to the Bull: hence the chaotic state of the hotel bills that were presented to the other guests, and the mix-up about Wakeford's — which the prosecution attempted to attribute to the additional costs of his supposed companion. More significant was Blunden's discovery that the accounts clerk had been living in the hotel for the whole time of the Archdeacon's first visit to Peterborough. It is possible, as Blunden believed, that this was the woman who Harold Osborne claimed that he saw taking breakfast with the Pughs on the morning of the 15th March 1920. It would then only be necessary for Pugh's friend obligingly to have added Wakeford to the scene he remembered or, conceivably, to have been genuinely mistaken in his identification — especially when Osborne was recalling events that took place more than a year before.

Like so many things about the Wakeford Case, it is the sheer improbability that sticks in the gullet: the picture of the Archdeacon of Stow breakfasting in a private room with his doxy, sitting at the same table with the seedy manager of a commercial hotel and his shrill wife. Add to this the fact that the manager and his wife did not mention this startling event in their evidence — while witness after reliable witness swore that John Wakeford took breakfast in the grill room that morning — and the improbability becomes absurd. Yet Harold Osborne's story was accepted by the Lord Chancellor and the other law lords, as in the end was the whole ram-shackle edifice, assembled by Agar and added to by Wright, at the core of which lay the inconsistencies, inaccuracies, perjuries and downright lies of the Peterborough police, Tuplin and the Pughs, about which Birkenhead spoke in such scathing terms. Yet it was enough to ruin the Archdeacon.

That John Wakeford was innocent is, in the last analysis, almost irrelevant, for his enemies genuinely believed him to be what they wished him to be: a lecher and a hypocrite. C.T. Moore and Herbert Worthington certainly had no qualms about their part in Wakeford's ruin. For them, the court

183

verdicts confirmed the correctness of their actions in exposing immorality in a man whose duty it was to be beyond suspicion.

There can, of course, be no absolute certainty about the inner life of any man and it is impossible rigidly to exclude the hypothesis that Wakeford was morally schizoid and a clandestine womaniser, as his enemies so firmly believed. If the events at Peterborough were the best evidence they could muster, their beliefs were ill-founded. Wakeford was a handsome and compelling man who could win the hearts and minds of those about him. But those who knew him best could never entertain the possibility that he was guilty.

In retrospect, Wakeford's downfall seems almost inevitable. He was an all-or-nothing man, a storm petrel who could evoke the strongest passions in those who knew him. To his enemies he was always an outsider: a jumped-up policeman's son with his autocratic pseudo-Catholic ways. He was an impulsive and, in some ways, a foolish man, but he was brave and steadfast and an intrepid fighter. His enemies approached him by stealth and subterfuge, and though he thrashed about clumsily in their net, Moore and Worthington and Fry destroyed him.

ACKNOWLEDGMENTS

Not least of the pleasures in writing this book was the help and friendship that I received from many people in tracing the life and times of Archdeacon Wakeford. I am particularly grateful to Brigadier John Wakeford and Major Aubrey Moore for speaking so openly and hospitably to a complete stranger about some delicate family matters.

A culminating excitement in my researches was the discovery of Freda Hansen, sixty-five years after the events described in this book. She had concealed even from her own family that she was the 'Girl in the Cathedral' and I am therefore deeply appreciative that she agreed to relate to me her part in the affair.

I am also indebted to those who helped me reconstruct John Wakeford's early years in Devon. Notably, Arthur Salter and Alfred Wigmore who talked to me about Devonport dockyard in Victorian times, Michael Manisty of Harberton Manor, who loaned me photographs of and talked about Archdeacon Earle, and Edward Manisty who gave me access to the Earle papers. Fred Baker provided invaluable help with his

185

reminiscences of the Worthington and Woolcombe families at Northlew and Ashbury at the turn of the century. I was also assisted by the staffs of the Devonport Dockyard Museum, the Devon Record Office, the Diocesan Registry at Exeter, the Plymouth City Library and, in Sussex, by Patricia Gill, of the West Sussex Record Office, and Mary Hobbs of the Cathedral office at Chichester.

At Liverpool, I received exceptional kindness from the present Vicar of St Margaret's, Anfield, Bernard Elsdon, and much patient help from his parishioners, especially Margaret Foxcroft and Ethel Grogan, who still remember John Wakeford. I am indebted to James Brophy for talking with me about St Margaret's School and to the present headmaster for providing me with photocopies of Mr Brophy's history of the school; I am also grateful to the Church Council of St Margaret's for permission to borrow the last traceable set of the *St Margaret's Review* covering Wakeford's years at Anfield and to Philip Waller, of Merton College, for clarifying some confusing episodes in the Liverpool history. It is a pleasure to acknowledge the cheerful assistance of Miss Organ of the Liverpool Record Office.

At Lincoln, I was privileged to receive the help, advice and friendship of Fred Morton, for many years reporter and then chief reporter of the *Lincolnshire Echo*. It is sad that Fred did not live to see the publication of this book in which he took so much interest. I am also greatly indebted to Michael Allison of Nettleham: there were few enquiries concerning cathedral life at Lincoln in the early decades of the century which could not be swiftly settled by a telephone call to Nettleham. I benefited from a correspondence with Frank Newcomb of Gainsborough, from the generosity of Horace Drake in lending me the papers of the late Austin Lee — a Lincolnshire parson, writer and son of the rectory in Wakeford's archdeaconry — and from the help of Betty Denby, whose mother, the late Lily Cooke, was in service at the Precentory in Wakeford's time. I am also grateful to Derek

186

Winterbottom, Dean Fry's biographer, and to Trisilian Nicholas, of Trinity College, one of Fry's last surviving pupils at Berkhamsted, for their views on Archdeacon Wakeford's principal adversary at Lincoln, and to Joan Williams, of the cathedral library, for her unstinting help. The staff of the Lincoln Central Library provided invaluable assistance.

My researches at Netherseal and Appleby Magna were made pleasurable by the friendship of William Bate and his parishioners, particularly by that gentle and kindly man the late Bill Woodward. In my visits to Peterborough, I was helped by Richard Paton and by Oshor Osib, who not only gave me the free run of The Bull Hotel but provided liberal refreshments; by Martin Howe, the Museum Services Curator, and the staff of the Peterborough Reference Library. I am grateful to Anna McKenzie, of the Inner London Probation Service, for tracing Elspeth Gray who talked to me about Evelyn Porter, and to Donald Foubister for reminiscing about Margaret Tyler. I am especially indebted to Claire Blunden and Barry Webb who spoke to me about Edmund Blunden; to David Owen and Donald Rushton for receiving me at the offices of the Privy Council, and educating me about the history of the Judicial Committee. Kevin Brownlow and Elaine Burrows, of the National Film Archives, helped me in my search for the Gaumont film on the Wakeford Case, and John Wrottesley generously shared his encyclopaedic knowledge of the Great Northern Railway.

My attempt to reconstruct Wakeford's declining years at Biggin Hill was made possible by the assistance of Gilbert Smith, John Nelson, Tom Temple, Raymond Forbes, the Gooding brothers of Polesteeple House and Elizabeth Silverthorn of the Borough Library at Bromley. I am also indebted to the staffs of the British Library, the Newspaper Library at Colindale, Cambridge University Library, Cambridge City Library and the local history sections of the public libraries at Birmingham, Camden, Leicester and

Nottingham.

Finally, I thank the College friends whom I plagued during the writing of this book, especially David Lloyd Jones, who read the manuscript, and Tim Briden, Charles Harpum, John Hopkins and Stanley French. Above all, I am deeply indebted to Paul Chipchase, who not only suggested that I should write this book, but nursed me through bouts of literary depression and patiently read, and greatly improved, each of the chapters as they were written — and to Margaret Clements who typed them so beautifully.

★   ★   ★

I acknowledge the following sources of illustrations: Plate 1, Brigadier J.C. Wakeford; Plate 2, Devon Library Services; Plate 3, photograph by Browning of Exeter; Plate 4, painting by A.S. Cope; Plates 5 and 6, Mr Fred Baker; Plate 7, W. & A.H. Fry, Ltd.; Plate 8, Miss Margaret Foxcroft; Plate 9, Liverpool City Libraries; Plate 10, Lincolnshire Library Service; Plates 11 and 13, Lincoln Cathedral Library; Plate 12, Mrs Betty Denby; Plate 14, author's photograph; Plate 15, Major Aubrey Moore; Plate 16, Mr William Woodward; Plate 17, Peterborough Museum Services; Plate 18, Dr Simon Maddrell; Plates 19 and 20, The Press Association; Plates 21, 22, 23, 26 and 27, BBC Hulton Picture Library; Plate 24, Mrs Claire Blunden; Plate 28, Mrs Doreen Winslade.

BIBLIOGRAPHY

BOOKS AND BOOKLETS

Aglionby, F.E., *The Life of Edward Henry Bickersteth D.D. Bishop and Poet*, Longmans, Green, London, 1907

Blunden, Edmund, *John Clare: Beginner's Luck*, Bridge Books, Kent Editions, 1971

Brophy, James, *The Story of St Margaret's Boys School*, Anfield, 1976

Burrows, Roland (ed.), *Judgements Delivered by Lord Chancellor Birkenhead 1919-1920*, H.M.S.O., 1923

Burns, K.V., *The Devonport Dockyard Story*, Maritime Books, Duloe, Cornwall, 1984

Bunch, Allan (ed.), *Old Peterborough in Photographs*, Peterborough Museum and Art Gallery, 1979

Campbell, John, *F.E. Smith, First Earl of Birkenhead*, Cape, London, 1983

Colvin, Ian, *The Life of Lord Carson* (3 vols), Gollancz, London, 1936

Fowler, J.H., *The Life and Letters of Edward Lee Hicks* (Bishop of Lincoln 1910-1919), Christophers, London, 1922

Furneaux, Rupert, 'A Cause so Perilous. The Trial of

Archdeacon Wakeford' in *Society Scandals* (ed. Bridgeman, Harriet and Drury, Elizabeth), David & Charles, Newton Abbot, 1977

Graves, Robert and Hodge, Alan, *The Long Week-End: A Social History of Great Britain 1918-1919*, Four Square, London, 1961

Greene, Graham, *A Sort of Life*, Bodley Head, London, 1971

Griffiths, R., *Life of Pastor George Wise*, Toxteth, 1909

Hanbury, Robert, *The Wakeford Appeal: An Examination of the Judgement and a Defence of the Archdeacon*, Sutton, Surrey, 1921

Heuston, R.F.V., *Lives of the Lord Chancellors, 1888-1940*, Clarendon Press, Oxford, 1964

Hyde, H. Montgomery, *Carson*, Constable, London, 1974

Mallon, Thomas, *Edmund Blunden*, Twayne Publishers, Boston, 1983

Mitchell, C. Ainsworth, *A Scientist in the Criminal Courts*, Chapman & Hall, London, 1945

Moore, Aubrey, *Son of the Rectory: from Leicestershire to the Somme*, Sutton, Gloucester, 1982

Muir, Dorothy Erskine, *Lift the Curtain*, Cape, London, 1955

Nelson, John, *Grandfather's Biggin Hill*, Biggin Hill, 1982

Pilley, W. Charles, *The Mystery of the Wakeford Case*, *John Bull*, London, 1922

Rhodes, H.T.F., *The Craft of Forgery*, Murray, London, 1934

Sandford, E.G. (ed.), *Memoirs of Archbishop Temple by Seven Friends*, Vols I and II, Macmillan, London, 1906

Sandford, E.G., *The Exeter Episcopate of Archbishop Temple*, Macmillan, London, 1907

Stephens, W.R.W., *A Memoir of Richard Durnford, D.D.*, Murray, London, 1899

Swayne, W.S., *Parson's Pleasure*, Blackwood, Edinburgh, 1934

Symons, Julian, *Horatio Bottomley*, Crescent Press, London, 1955

Taylor, H.A., *Smith of Birkenhead*, Stanley Paul, London,

1928

'M.L.T.', *Was Archdeacon Wakeford Impersonated?* Bale & Danielsson, London, 1921

Wakeford, John, *Rural Missions*, Griffith & Farran, London, 1888

Wakeford, John, *The Finding of the Cross*, Treacher, Brighton, 1890

Wakeford, John, *Priesthood & Priestcraft*, Faith Press, London, 1920

Wakeford, John, *Not Peace but a Sword: A Biography*, John Wakeford, Biggin Hill, 1925

Waller, P.J., *Democracy and Sectarianism: A Political and Social History of Liverpool 1868-1939*, Liverpool University Press, 1981

Whitfield, H.F., *Plymouth and Devonport: In Times of War and Peace*, Chapple, Plymouth, 1900

Winterbottom, Derek, *Doctor Fry*, Berkhamsted, 1977

Woodward, Reg, *Boy on a Hill*, Grantham, 1984

Worth, R.N., *History of Devonport*, Plymouth, 1890

MANUSCRIPTS, LETTERS AND PAPERS

Alfred Earle papers (in the possession of Mr Edward Manisty)

'Memoirs 1895-1920' by E.F.R. Woolley (ms. in Lincoln Cathedral Library)

Letters of the Reverend James Penney, 1914-15 (Lincolnshire Archives Office)

'Adultery in Gaiters' by Austin Lee (ms. in the possession of Mr Horace Drake)

'History of the Dockyard Police' by Alfred Wigmore (ms. at H.M. Dockyard, Devonport)

Asquith mss. 22, folio 51 (Bodleian Library, Oxford)

List of the case papers for Wakeford's Consistory Court Trial (Lincolnshire Archives Office)

BIBLIOGRAPHY

NEWSPAPERS, MAGAZINES AND PERIODICALS

The Bioscope
*The British Homeopathic
Journal*
Bromley and Kentish Times
Bromley Mercury
Chichester Diocesan Kalendar
The Church Times
Daily Dispatch
Daily Express
Daily Herald
Daily Mail
Daily News
Daily Sketch
Daily Telegraph
East Anglian Times
Folkestone Express
John Bull

Kentish Times
The Law Quarterly Review
Leicester Mercury
Lincoln Diocesan Calendar
The Lincolnshire Chronicle
The Lincolnshire Echo
Liverpool Daily Post
Liverpool Echo
Liverpool Mercury
The Liverpool Review
The Nation and the Athenaeum
Peterborough Advertiser
St Margaret's Review
Sunday Express
The Times
The Westminster Gazette